Organizing the Culture of Death:

Using congregations for progressive politics through Alinskyian organizing

By Stephanie Block

Table of Contents

What have I gotten myself into? 1

Saul Alinsky's experiments with community organizing 4

Alinskyian organizing in the churches (Catholic) 8

Funding the organizing: the Catholic Campaign for Human Development 12

Organizing and Funding in other Religious Institutions 21

Liberationism and a Marxist Worldview (Re-educating the Believer) 32

We Are Not Grassroots.. 39

Progressive Politics 45

Education "reform" 50

Healthcare "reform" 57

Shaping the media message (Faith in Public Life) 62

Tactical Manipulation 66

A Closing Thought... 71

When my husband took a job in New Mexico as a music professor, he also became the organist for a small Catholic parish.

Bart and Frances sang in the "Glory and Praise" choir. Frances may only stand at 4'8" but she's formidable – related to half the population of Albuquerque's South Valley (including Bart, many generations back) and is on friendly terms with the other half.

So, when the parish was assigned a new priest from Chicago who had been trained in Alinskyian organizing, he pegged Frances and Bart as potential "leaders." They were smart, active, and influential. He asked them to help him start a new "ministry" in the parish.

Father was a little vague about what that ministry was, exactly. They'd just have to "come and see."

The "come and see" took the form of a meeting in a parish classroom, run by a fellow who said he was beginning a new organization in the city. Our parish would be part of that organization and so would other congregations, including Presbyterians and Methodists and Lutherans and Episcopalians. They'd come together and hold house-meetings to discuss neighborhood problems and then act together to fix those problems.

Everyone at the "come and see" was enthusiastic… except Frances. She knew a little about radicals. Her parents had owned a small restaurant in the university area when she was young. During the student unrest of the 60s and early 70s, it was targeted by Brown Berets – a Chicano Liberation movement – who harassed them for free food.

Frances' parents were generous people, who often slipped an extra burrito into a hungry freshman's order, but they were not going to be exploited by swaggering, self-important hoodlums. Frances watched the marches through the restaurant window and heard the insults hurled against her parents for their "traitorous capitalism." It did not leave a good taste in her mouth.

Something about this "come and see" had a similar "odor" to it. She asked if there was any material she could read about the type of organizing being proposed and was given several titles, including Saul Alinsky's *Rules for Radicals*.

Unfortunately, *Rules for Radicals* was out of print at this time so she called my husband to see if he could find a copy in the university library.

He did…and we spent the next several days on the phone, me reading and Frances squealing with horror.

The *Rules* began with an opening "dedication:"

> Lest we forget at least an over-the-shoulder acknowledgment to the very first radical; from all our legends, mythology, and history (and who is to know where mythology leaves off and history begins - or which is which), the first radical

known to man who rebelled against the establishment and did it so effectively that he at least won his own kingdom - Lucifer.

These were disturbing words, whatever Alinsky meant by them. The opening pages of chapter one were no better.

> What follows is for those who want to change the world from what it is to what they believe it should be. *The Prince* was written by Machiavelli for the Haves on how to hold power. *Rules for Radicals* is written for the Have-Nots on how to take it away.

Nicolò Machiavelli published his notorious work on statecraft, *Il Principe* (*The Prince*) in the 16th century. It was written to assist his patrons in cold-blooded, practical methods for expanding and retaining political power. Machiavelli taught that the interests of the state supersede all others, including the moral law.

He says, for example:

> So you see a wise ruler cannot, and should not, keep his word when doing so is to his disadvantage, and when the reasons that led him to promise to do so no longer apply. Of course, if all men were good, this advice would be bad; but since men are wicked and will not keep faith with you, you need not keep faith with them…But it is essential to know how to conceal how crafty one is, to know how to be a clever counterfeit and hypocrite.

The book was condemned by the Church and placed on its Index of Forbidden Texts in 1559 for its bald-faced embrace of the "Culture of Death", though different terms were used at the time.

Four hundred years later, Alinsky paid his debt to Machiavelli's thought by writing in *Rules for Radicals*:

· The third rule of the ethics of means and ends is that … the end justifies almost any means. (p. 29)

· All effective actions require the passport of morality. (p. 44)

· The seventh rule of the ethics of means and ends is that generally success or failure is a mighty detriment of ethics ... There can be no such thing as a successful traitor, for if one succeeds, he becomes a founding father. (p. 34)

· The tenth rule of the ethics of means and ends is that you do what you can with what you have and clothe it with moral garments. ... Moral rationalization is indispensable at all tunes of action whether to justify the selection or the use of ends or means. (p. 36)

· An organizer working for change ... does not have a fixed truth - truth to him is relative and changing. (p. 10-11)

Of course, Alinsky has developed each of these ideas (and others) at length, but their explanations render them even *more* objectionable, not less. They are the very antithesis of Christian ethics.

There was also this business of Haves and Have-Nots, locked in perpetual battle over the stuff they have or don't have, which Alinsky proposes to *exacerbate* with his tactical weapons. Catholics have a large, developed body of social teaching and that isn't the way the Church looks at things.   The poor and the wealthy are equal under God's judgment and are both called to charity. It's a very different approach to the problem of poverty.

Back to Frances. We located a few more copies of *Rules for Radicals* in a used bookstore near campus and by the second organizational meeting, Frances had her own copy, which she brought with her and placed on the table, it's bright red cover lying face up.   Father saw it and walked over, his face dark.

"What's this? McCarthyism?"

Where had *that* remark come from? No one had mentioned Marxism.

Since the 2008 election, there is greater awareness about the influence Saul Alinsky on several prominent, contemporary politicians but little appreciation for the breadth of damage wrecked by the organizations he created.

Alinsky was a pioneer of community organizing who authored two seminal books on the subject: *Reveille for Radicals* (1946) and *Rules for Radicals* (1971). He was born in Chicago, Illinois on January 30, 1909 and educated at the University of Chicago, from which he graduated with a doctorate in criminology, studying the local mafia and unions. These latter groups schooled him in the practical tactics of manipulation and power.

Alinsky's first major organizing effort was in the Chicago slums of the late 1930s. With the help of Bishop Bernard Sheil, a senior auxiliary bishop in the Diocese of Chicago who was highly supportive of the labor movement (and who probably saw neighborhood organizing as a logical extension), Alinsky brought together disparate ethnic factions in his *Back of the Yards Neighborhood Council*. This collaboration developed enough clout to win major concessions from the meatpacking company that owned the Chicago stockyards and which was largely responsible for the neighborhood's livelihood, as well as for many aspects of its wretchedness.

The backbone of Alinsky's organizational principles is that power comes from money or from large numbers of organized people. *Reveille for Radicals* taught that the "the answer to all of the issues facing us will be found in the masses of the people themselves, and *nowhere else*," (p. 40, emphasis in original) and that "we know to date most of our pain, frustration, defeat, and failure has come from using an imperfect instrument, a partial democracy." (p. 39)

After *Back of the Yards*, Alinsky organized in other cities, hiring and training fellow radicals in his brutally pragmatic approach to organizing. He taught them to treat opponents "...not as persons but as symbols representing ideas or interests which he believes inimical to the welfare of the people." (p. 18) "Radicals precipitate the social crisis by action," "...radicals rebel...," (p. 22) "[the radical] will realize that in the initial stages of organization he must deal with the qualities of ambition and self-interest as realities. Only a fool would step into a community dominated by materialistic standards and self-interest and begin to preach ideals." (p. 92) "Self-interest", therefore, became the bait by which organizers drew people into working with them.

Alinsky's theories are predicated on the Marxist notion of class conflict, as made evident from his simplistic division of the world into Haves, Have-A-Little Want-Mores, and Have-Nots.

> The despair is there; now it's up to us to go in and rub raw the sores of discontent, galvanize them for radical social change. ... We'll start with specific issues -- taxes, jobs, consumer problems, pollution - and from there move on to the larger issues: pollution in the Pentagon and the Congress and the board rooms of the megacorporations. Once you

organize people, they'll keep advancing from issue to issue toward the ultimate objective: people power."[1]

Alinsky believed that a neighborhood "people's organization" was a practical school of democracy. His citizenship classes, using popular education techniques (*Reveille for Radicals*, chapter 9), were seen as an essential component of citizen development to enable participation in the creation of societal change.

Alinsky's own people's organization, the Industrial Areas Foundation, which was founded in 1940, is today a national umbrella for over 70 affiliate broad-based organizations around the United States and the world. There are other networks of related affiliate organizations that have sprung from his theories and "principles," too, including PICO (Pacific Institute for Community Organizing), Gamaliel, and DART (Direct Action and Research Training Institute).

Alinsky experimented with several models of organizing. One model allows for only **institutional membership** – that is, only an entire congregation, a school, a union, a healthcare facility, or another community organization can join. This means, of course, that every individual within a member institution "belongs" to the Alinskyian people's organization and is counted as supporting whatever political position , public policy, or program the people's organization is promoting.

When the institutions are predominantly congregations, the organizing is said to be **faith-based**. Where it involves a wide range of secular institutions, as well, it is said to be **broad-based**.

All these models – institutional or individual membership, broad-based or faith-based – have their strengths and weaknesses. Alinsky came to prefer the faith-based model because it provided the necessary "moral garment" for his work in the most efficient manner. According to Ed Chambers, the lead organizer trained by Alinsky to take over the Industrial Areas Foundation upon his death:

> The Industrial Areas Foundation (Alinsky Institute) has been in the field of organizing for nearly forty years. We believe that the best hope for change and social justice is the Church (The Judeo-Christian tradition).
>
> The churches have the networks, the relationship of loyalty and trust, the money, the values and the untapped talent of the people...
>
> [The organization] is a commitment to process and empowerment rather than task or service. It's grounded in the real world rather than the world as it should be (self-interest vs altruism). It's pragmatic with aimed, calculated, deliberate action.

---

[1] Playboy Interview with Saul Alinsky, "Empowering People, Not Elites," March 1972

It does not wallow in conferences, resolutions or ideological refinements. It acts to win.

...It initiates fights on those issues that are immediate, specific and winnable. The developing leaders learn to personalize and polarize. They learn to analyze, evaluate and judge what they are doing and how they are acting..."

As Alinsky and the organizers he trained honed their efforts, they developed an approach that is used fairly consistently across the networks. Organizers generally begin a new affiliate by analyzing where they would like to have a presence. What area of a state or in the country will increase their political leverage?

They then identify institutional heads who have a progressive reputation. Those who are interested in a new, political venture must permit **one-on-ones** – interviews with individuals within their institutions – to be conducted. A core of people with the "right" brand of civic interest and the capacity to rally another dozen or so people to meetings is chosen for **leadership training**.

House meetings encourage discussion about the issues the Alinskyian organization wants to tackle. The meetings are designed to produce specific outcomes and discourage others, according to what is most advantageous for the affiliate. They give the organization the ability to say that it has spoken with hundreds (or thousands) of local people and that *everyone* is interested and concerned about those issues.

During its formative years, the organization may go by one name which is then changed at an official **launch-event**. However, the organizational work of identifying and training new leadership, along with the neighborhood presence created by house meetings, is essential to the organization's continued growth. It will go on for the life of each affiliate.

Actions can include all sorts of things. Periodic **assemblies** ratify the actions that organizers and leaders predetermine. These actions may include rallies, marches, or **accountability** nights, where politicians are asked to voice their assent to the organization's desired policy, legislation, or program. No dissent or discussion is permitted at these events. They aren't democratic debates but orchestrated rituals to give participants a sense of ownership in the organization's agenda and to discourage politicians from expressing public opposition.

These actions operate on several levels. Local, "**winnable**" projects serve to identify and train leadership, eliminate those with whom it would be difficult to work, and build relationships and trust among various factions. They are not the *ultimate* goal of the organization, which is radical social change, although the precise "social changes" being sought are seldom defined.

Sometimes these local, winnable projects will, in a small way, support that ultimate goal – for example, projects that support the creation of a fully integrated, national education-workforce system – but other projects are entirely benign and unobjectionable, *per se*. They are nevertheless useful for training new leadership and building relationships of trust for the organization.

The great social upheaval of the 1960s took place, underground, for some time before bursting out into "mainstream" awareness. Its US roots lay, in part, with the Protestant "social gospel" movement of the late 19th century and the Catholic "liberation theology" movement that began in the mid-twentieth century among European intellectuals and spread to impoverished areas of Latin America. The common denominator of both movements is a false historicity,[2] a reinterpretation of the Christian faith through an economic-political lens, and a flirtation – if not open marriage – with socialism.

The US Catholic Church witnessed the first major, public assault against its authority during a three-day *Call to Action* Conference in Detroit in October 1976, which had been sponsored by the *National Conference of Catholic Bishops*. This Conference brought together delegates from across the United States to ratify eight position papers that had been prepared in advance.[3]

Several of these papers had the clear imprint of Saul Alinsky's *Industrial Areas Foundation* (IAF) on them. For example, the working paper on *Neighborhood* recommended (and it was approved by the *Call to Action* delegates) that every parish support a "competent," ecumenical neighborhood action group, with diocesan resources used to train organizational "leaders" for their use.[4] The IAF had also been involved the year before in a pre-Detroit "hearing" on the topic of *Nationhood*. The *Nationhood* working papers subsequently proposed that the Church establish priorities for public policy, define major election issues, educate the laity on the moral dimensions of public issues, and implement these goals ecumenically, that is, in conjunction with other religions and civic groups.

Monsignor Jack Egan of Chicago, "a longtime Alinsky supporter, IAF board member, and activist on Chicago urban issues,"[5] served as co-chair of the 1976 Call to Action plenary sessions. [6] The Call to Action "working papers" contained specific challenges to the discipline and doctrine of the Church. "…[M]ore than 2,400 delegates at the conference - people deeply involved in the life of the institutional church and appointed by their bishops – approve such progressive resolutions, ones calling for, among other things, the ordination of women and

---

[2] Various thinkers in these movements accuse the Christian churches not only of indifference toward the plight of the poor, but of a class-based alignment with the rich and powerful coupled with "pie in the sky" theology. While one can, of course, find examples of such abuses throughout its 2000 year history, the Church has been one of mankind's most powerful *earthly* advocates.

[3] The position papers were on the topics of 1) Nationhood, 2) Neighborhood, 3) Family, 4) Humankind, 5) Personhood, 6) Ethnicity, 7) Church, and 8) Work. They are described in a number of places, one being the *Call to Action* "Working Papers: Introduction," NCCB, undated (circa 1976).

[4] 1976 *Call to Action* working paper on "Nationhood," p. 12, l. 13-17.

[5] *The Neighborhood Works, op.cit.*

[6] Heidi Schlumpf, "Remembering the First Call to Action Conference," *The New World News*, September 20, 1996.

married men, female altar servers, and the right and responsibility of married couples to form their own consciences on the issue of artificial birth control."[7]

Obviously, the hierarchy of the Catholic Church was in no position to ratify these proposals but it has been the effort of *Call to Action*-related organizations, including the IAF, each within its own sphere of influence, to bring about the changes it could.   For example, in the years after the 1976 inaugural *Call to Action* Conference, it may not yet be that *every* United States Catholic parish supports a "competent," ecumenical neighborhood-action group, with diocesan and parish resources used to train organizational "leaders," but there are scores of IAF – and PICO, Gamaliel, DART, etc. – affiliates in cities around the United States, most of which have a number of Catholic parishes among their members. These affiliates receive Catholic money through an annual "poverty appeal" called the *Catholic Campaign for Human Development* (CCHD) and through the **dues**[8] of their member parishes. [9]

No closer to solving the problem of poverty, CCHD continues to fund Alinskyian organizing with the sales pitch that it is "breaking the cycle of poverty."[10]   Call to Action continues to be a functioning movement with the American Catholic Church, lobbying for the same "reforms" it attempted to coerce the Church into accepting in 1976.   There's been a lot of damage to the Church during those many years.

So far, we've only been speaking of Catholic history. There is a similar story to tell in each of the mainstream Protestant denominations.

The Evangelical Lutheran Church in America (ELCA) was born in 1987, the product of various splits and realignments among the US Lutheran population.[11]   According to a *Faith in Public Life*[12] document, "Community Organizing and National Denominations," almost immediately after its inception the ELCA began meeting with members of the larger, national organizing networks. From these discussions, the ELCA developed a six-point strategic plan on the integration of faith-based organizing throughout the denomination, hoping "to produce a powerful force that can act as a real agent of social change." [13]

The four major Alinskyian networks are all involved in the project – the Industrial Areas Foundation, founded by Saul Alinsky, and DART, Gamaliel, and PICO, whose founding organizers learned their craft at Alinsky's feet. The *Faith in Public Life* document explains that "[t]he ultimate goal of this effort is to change the culture of the church so that community organizing is an integral part of every congregation of the ELCA."

---

[7] *The New World News*, op. cit.

[8] Member institutions are accessed a percentage – often 1.5 % - of their annual income.

[9] The larger IAF-style networks are PICO (Pacific Institute for Community Organization), DART (Direct Action and Research Training Center), and the Gamaliel Foundation. There are other, smaller networks, as well.

[10] CCHD newsletter letterhead: "Helping People Help Themselves: breaking the cycle of poverty for over 40 years," 2015, issue one.

[11] www.elca.org carries a detailed history

[12] See chapter 13.

[13] www.faithinpubliclife.org/content/case-studies/partnerships_between_national.html; The ELCA has a website for those interested in its organizing efforts: www.elca.org/organizing/index.html

It is hardly coincidental that at the same time the ELCA has been moving toward the goal of reinventing itself as an earthly "agent of social change," the denomination has been changing doctrinally, too. Official positions on homosexuality – expressing the traditional, Biblical belief that marriage is between a man and woman, that homosexual erotic activity is sinful, and that people leading homosexually active lives cannot hold positions of ministry – have been shifting over the last two decades.

Naturally, the newly organized ELCA will bring its new moral values into the public – and political – arena.

According to the same *Faith in Public Life* document, the **Presbyterian Church (USA)** has signed a joint statement with the ELCA concerning plans to get more involved nationally with local community organizing. It's a fascinating position paper,[14] the product of a national gathering coordinated by the Urban Ministry Office of the Presbyterian Church (USA) and the Congregation-based Community Organizing/Leadership Development for Public Life Office of the Evangelical Lutheran Church in America. It observes that congregation-based (faith-based) community organizing, already an established fact in many congregations, has "proven to be a revitalizing strategy for congregations and expands the reach and vision of ministry." It therefore advocates that each denomination increase funding for organizing and explore the ways it "can be a vital part of congregational re-development and new church development.... working together with other denominations on a national strategy around public policy using a community organizing framework."

For seminarians, there is the particular recommendation to "engage in appropriate learning projects related to congregation-based community organizing. Faculties of seminaries [should] be encouraged to provide resources to the larger church of the theological and biblical foundations of social justice through a CBCO [congregation-based community organizing] strategy."

Lastly, congregations are to employ "the strategies of community organizing – individual meetings, house meetings, building a relational culture – for congregational transformation....[u]sing CBCO as a primary strategy for mission, understanding its systemic approach as compared to direct service or advocacy."

Rabbi Jonah Presner is a *Faith in Public Life* spokesman who serves the *Industrial Areas Foundation* (IAF) network as co-chair of its Boston IAF affiliate and also as the director of *Just Congregations*, a social action program developed by the **Union of Reform Judaism** to train Jewish congregations across the country in IAF-based organizing. *Just Congregations* provides the "language and organizing out of their faith tradition," as "the language of Christianity, in

---

[14] "Lutheran—Presbyterian Congregation-based Community Organizing Consultation," signed October 13-15, 2005, www.interfaithfunders.org/PresbandLutherans.html.

particular, can make Jews uncomfortable and hesitant to participate. Exacerbating these feelings can be conflicting positions by the two faiths on issues such as abortion and gay rights."[15]

Like the *Catholic Campaign for Human Development,* there is a Jewish funding mechanism for faith-based organizing – the *Jewish FundS for Justice* (JFSJ). The Just Congregations Initiative would support several JFSJ projects: recruiting synagogue leaders for the national gathering; engaging clergy in the CBCO [congregation-based community organizing] task force, connecting leaders locally to JFSJ initiatives; and encouraging [seminary] faculty and students to support and attend CBCO seminary training sessions…. most importantly, the Union/Just Congregations staff members would coordinate a national strategy together with JFSJ staff to determine together which geographic regions are ripe to be targeted for Reform Jewish engagement in CBCO.[16]

---

[15] Daniel Levisohn, Assistant Editor, JTNews: "Faith Alliance reaches out to Jewish congregations," www.jtnews.net/index.php?/news/item/899

[16] urj.org/justcongregations/jfsj

The Catholic Campaign for Human Development [CCHD] is an annual collection of the United States Catholic Conference of Bishops. The *United States Catholic Conference* launched the collection in 1970 under the name of the *Campaign for Human Development* with three purposes. The first and best understood of these is the funding of economic self-help projects run by the poor as a way of addressing domestic poverty.

[C]CHD's[17] founding resolution stated that "the magnitude and complexity of poverty in the U.S. in a time of rapid social change...calls for the creation of a new source of financial capital that can be allocated for specific social projects aimed at eliminating the very causes of poverty....There is an evident need for funds designated to be used for organized groups of white and minority poor to develop economic strength and political power in their own community...."

Secondly, the collection was intended to fund educational programs that would raise the level of awareness among middle and upper classes for the plight of the poor. The founding resolution committed the Campaign to "lead the People of God to a new knowledge of today's problems, a deeper understanding of the intricate forces that lead to group conflict, and a perception of some new and promising approaches that we might take in promoting a greater spirit of solidarity…"

The campaign's third purpose was to support social change. To bring that about, one third to over a half of [C]CHD grants have been used to fund Alinsky-style, broad-based community organizations.[18]

Besides training their membership to take civic action, these groups seek a fundamental restructuring of:
- Government,
- Education,
- Job training and placement,
- Healthcare,
- Housing, and
- Social service provision.

They are theologically liberationist. This means a number of problematic things. Liberationism fosters the idea of "class struggle" rather than the Christian values of solidarity and brotherhood.

Unlike Christianity, which teaches that moral truth is fixed in the nature of creation and is unchanging, liberationism operates from a consensualized "truth," that is, from the idea that "truth" and "morality" are determined by what people believe rather than being objective realities. Therefore, "morality" can be changed. It's this belief in a consensualized "truth" that

---

[17] When the collection was founded, it was called the *Campaign for Human Development* (CHD). After the first attempt to reform the collection, its name was changed to the *Catholic Campaign for Human Development* (CCHD). When speaking about events over a time period that spanned both names, the acronym is [C]CHD.
[18] These conservative figures are based on analysis of published CCHD national grants from 1992-2014. The amount of actual money represented by these percentages is about $2-3 million annually, not including additional *local* CCHD grants.

enables an Alinskyian organization to claim it advocates "justice" while it ignores (or sustains) the injustice of intentionally killing a child in utero, for example.

Liberationism also politicizes the spiritual life, assessing imperfect, troubled economic or socio-political structures to be root *causes* of evil rather than a *consequence* of human actions, done by free and responsible persons. Rather than helping individuals to become stronger and more effective in their lives, the Alinskyian organization reeducates the individual to work for a society that will make it unnecessary to develop personal virtues or resources.

The educational programs of the [C]CHD are liberationist. An older CHD publication, "Sourcebook on Poverty, Development and Justice,"[19] produced by the CHD during the tenure of Sr. Josephine Dunne, SHCJ[20] (CHD Education Coordinator) is a collection of essays explaining the foundational liberation theology of the CHD and its preference for "liberating education." "Liberating education," for Dunne, was a process quite distinct from traditional western education, which she typed as "being institutional, self-serving and divorced from developmental needs, forcing the learned to look elsewhere for *meaning* and causing institutional education to be in many cases the experience of irrelevance. Catholic education in the U.S. seems to have shared in this deficiency."

In its stead, Dunne offered a "new theory of catechesis" that included values clarification and a threefold pedagogy, which she termed transference, reflection, and action-living (see-judge-act), lived out by the learner in a "continual dialectical interrelationship."

While see-judge-act methodology is not *necessarily* manipulative, liberationists have used it to lead participants to pre-determined conclusions. For example, later CCHD educational materials such as Session 1 of "Poverty and Faithjustice,"[21] guided the student through a see-judge-act pedagogy to "judge" that poverty can only be addressed by a fundamental change in the social and economic structures of the United States.

CCHD's current education program, JustFaith, continues the pattern. JustFaith presents very little in the way of *Catholic* social teaching. With its emphasis on *praxis* – on experiential formation rather than intellectual formation – an enormous amount of *its* "teaching" is accomplished within the context of emotional relationship, beginning with individual JustFaith groups and expanding to include JustFaith partners and the other activist organizations that JustFaith studies.

Not all activism is equal – obviously. JustFaith has made particular choices in its emphasis on studying the work of Alinskyian organizing networks or the Call to Action-related Pax Christi and other liberationist-oriented groups. Many of these groups do some good; they are not good models for Catholic Action, however.

This distinction between *Catholic* Action and other "doing good" isn't a matter of parochial chauvinism but of a very different way of understanding the human person and, therefore, of

---

[19] Education Staff of the Campaign for Human Development [Editors], "Sourcebook on Poverty, Development and Justice," 1972.
[20] Society of the Holy Child Jesus
[21] Catholic Campaign for Human Justice, "Poverty and Faithjustice: An Adult Education Program on Christian Discipleship in the United States," USCCB Publishing, 1998.

understanding human development. For instance, JustFaith never mentions, except as one of seven (flawed) themes, any of the life issues that are so pressing in contemporary society. It doesn't address any of the problems of the family, which the Church calls "the first natural society." It doesn't concern itself with marriage, which is the foundation of the family.

Nor does it understand that authentic human development is intimately and necessarily tied to the mission of the Church. That mission isn't to create perfect social, economic, or political structures but to bring the good news of God's salvific action among men. To the degree that they "get" that good news, the world will be a better place in which to live. To the degree that they miss it, the world will be a living hell.

When the goal is to move people into a desired action, there is a temptation to confuse the desired action with the principles behind it. To take a concrete example, in principle there is a limited "right to work." People need the means to earn a living and the dignity of being productive. However, all sorts of conditions circumscribe this "right." A penniless parent can't put his offspring into indentured servitude to pay the rent. The child's "right to work" is trumped by his "right to be educated," presuming, of course, that his "right to eat" has been met. It's a complicated world, out there.

Public programs to foster the "right to work" may also be complicated, taking in account certain factors and not others. Well-intentioned people, agreeing that, in principle, there is a "right to work" may nevertheless differ quite radically about how, in application, this is best accomplished.

JustFaith's encouragement to form "intentional" small communities that are aligned with the Alinskyian organizing networks or Pax Christi places them outside of the Church and into the roiling waters of liberationism and dissent. The small faith community is formed *outside* the Church but attempts to exert influence *inside* the Church that is contrary to Church teaching.

This is a big problem.

A biography about Msgr. Geno Baroni by journalist Lawrence M. O'Rouke, *Geno: The Life and Mission of Geno Baroni*, begins with a couple of notions that crystallize the great divide over what constitutes *social justice*. "It was no longer enough…to respond with charity to appeals for a food basket, the month's rent, or a bag of used underwear," O'Rouke writes about Father Baroni's vision for helping the poor. "The problems were too big for charity alone. Charity maintained people, but did not alter the system which locked them in their dismal place and exploited their weakness."[22]

Recognizing the reality of that statement isn't difficult for most people. However, determining which changes will "alter the system" for *good*, rather than for *ill*, is extremely contentious. Some "systemic" change is more reprehensible than the status quo it challenges, as anyone changing from a free state to enslavement will tell you. Furthermore, the *means* for accomplishing change must be considered, as well. What was the new system that Father

---

[22] Lawrence M. O'Rourke, *Geno: The Life and Mission of Gen Baroni*, (Paulist Press:1991), p. 3.

Baroni wanted to replace the flawed system of his time and how did he propose to accomplish the change?

The author's second comment that bears examination is: "Geno Baroni, a loyal priest in the Catholic faith, saw that his Church in America too often refused to recognize values in other religious faiths. He saw the potential strength of a concerned people sapped by unnecessary and self-destroying religious differences."[23]

Again, there's a legitimate way to understand such a remark and a problematic understanding. It's a fact that people living in the same polity share common concerns despite having different religious backgrounds. However, when amorphous, non-sectarian "religious values" are invoked to advance irreligious, political ambitions, there's great potential for abusing religion.

Father Geno Baroni's vision of social justice – the "systemic change" he sought and the "religious values" he believed would carry that change forward – was tremendously influential in setting the direction for Catholic activism in America. Between the late 1960s –1970s, Father Baroni was an advisor on national urban policy with the Carter administration and was president of the D.C.-based National Center for Urban Ethnic Affairs. He was a founding "architect" of the Catholic "social justice lobby" NETWORK,[24] and was among the priests who envisioned and pushed creation of the annual Campaign for Human Development (CHD) collection. He served on the Catholic Committee of Urban Ministry and was director of the Urban Taskforce of the United States Catholic Conference (USCC).

The organizations that he helped design – CHD and NETWORK, in particular – were *intended* to challenge the existing political system.[25] Supported by likeminded priests,[26] Father Baroni urged the 1969 Catholic bishops to create a fund "for human development"[27] that they adopted and understood *expressly* as a political instrument: "There is an evident need for funds designated to be used by organized groups of white and minority poor to develop...*political power* in their own communities."[28] [Emphasis added]

---

[23] *Geno,* p. 3.

[24] *Geno*, p 175-8; NETWORK is an organization run by Catholic religious women who are engaged in "progressive" political activism.

[25] Despite his best efforts, Baroni expressed frustration that "even the Campaign for Human Development was too wedded to the charities approach, that it failed to take risks on community organizers and developers who would challenge the political system." *Geno*, p. 258

[26] According to O'Rourke, Father Baroni invited these priests to meet in Combermere, Canada at the Madonna House Retreat Center, in August 1968, where they decided there needed to be a new approach to addressing poverty. *Geno*, p. 74. See also Marvin L. Krier Mich, Catholic Social Teaching and Movements (Twenty-Third Publications, 1998), p. 337-8.

[27] He and several others prepared a report, "Agenda for the 70s," that described the crisis and the need for a "new agenda." It called poverty the "greatest scandal of our affluent society," and asked several "moral questions," among them how might the Church "develop a spiritual response to meet our urban crisis?" The primary "response" suggested was the development of a national, Catholic fund for human development that would include an education component to develop "a domestic social consciousness." *Geno*, p. 74-83

[28] "Resolution on Crusade Against Poverty: A Resolution Adopted by the National Conference of Catholic Bishops," November 14, 1969.

Again, the language is vague and raises more questions than it answers. Who are these "organized groups"? What is the "political power" they amass intended to accomplish?

From the perspective of 45 years in the future, we can see where we've come but did the progressive priests and bishops who supported Father Baroni create what they intended?

It's O'Rouke's position that they were emphatically convinced that a *new system* of government, operating in partnership with community organizations that brokered the public largesse through mediating institutions, was the answer to "social welfare" problems. Father Baroni initially had "believed that government could do it all," but in the late 60s, observing the failure of Johnson's War on Poverty, "he began to wonder about the possibility of a cooperative effort involving government, the private sector, and the community."[29]

Many of the priests who worked with Father Baroni in the late 60s to create a fund for political activism, that is the CHD, "had been involved in or exposed to the Alinsky organization in Chicago and knew that the Church could support grassroots efforts to change urban public institutions….The Church could become a mediating institution, moving its resources to civil associations dedicated to fighting poverty and getting people civically engaged." [30]

The Church, serving as a secular "mediating institution" whose resources are under the control of other, secular entities with "civic", that is, with political, interests is quite a different proposition than an independent institution operating *outside* secular interests. One can't help but see an echo of Latin American and Asian efforts to co-opt the institutional Church for liberationist (i.e., for socialist) purposes, creating "people's churches" – the ironic name for "government churches – in its stead.

"People's churches" were never concerned about traditional expressions of the Faith – a personal relationship with God or personal morality – and certainly did not and do not support hierarchical authority. These "churches" viewed the world through the lens of class struggle and saw themselves as part of a revolutionary restructuring that included both governance and social structure.[31]

Poverty was therefore addressed in a classically socialist way – *not* by encouraging job growth or general economic growth, *not* by helping individuals to take greater personal responsibility or to learn more marketable skills but by managing more and more aspects of society, such as the educational system, the healthcare system, workforce development, and the like. "Urban planning" schemes failed, the thinking went, because they were too small. Society needed a bigger, more comprehensive plan.

How does one produce a "church" that will support this new structure? Like CHD, it was always about the Alinskyian community organizing.

---

[29] *Geno,* p. 74.
[30] Joseph M. Palacios, "The Catholic Social Imagination: Activism and the Just Society in Mexico and the United States," (University of Chicago Press, 2008), p. 91-2.
[31] Bonaventure Kloppenburg, OFM, *The People's Church*, Franciscan Herald Press, 1977.

Father Baroni, who – recall – was director of the USCC's Urban Taskforce, was also the "USCC's program director in the creation of the Calumet Community Congress in Gary, Indiana,"[32] and the Calumet Community Congress was set up by Saul Alinsky's Chicago-based Industrial Areas Foundation.[33]

The organization was short-lived. Democrats and Republicans of the time were unified in their discomfort over the new organization. "John Krupa, Lake County Democrat leader, called the Calumet Community Congress 'a power grab…motivated by the godless, atheistic forces of Communism.' Republican Rep. Earl Landgrebe said, 'One of the favorite tactics of Communists and other radical elements is to find a legitimate concern and take it over. There are strong indications that this is taking place in Lake County.'"[34]

"Its tone was angry, its behavior was assertive, and its anti-corporate philosophy was radical." [35] But, while it operated, it had support from the Bishop Andrew Grutka of Gary, Indiana, and, like any other Alinskyian community organization, had the financial backing of many local churches.

Baroni's "principles for social action" were a lot like Alinsky's. He saw the neighborhood as the building block for urban planning and the need for clergy participation in neighborhood organizations. One has to seize a crisis – or, if necessary, create one. And, most interestingly, he believed "that the role of the church in social action is to help convene people."[36]

> *"John Krupa, Lake County Democrat leader, called the Calumet Community Congress 'a power grab…motivated by the godless, atheistic forces of Communism.' Republican Rep. Earl Landgrebe said, 'One of the favorite tactics of Communists and other radical elements is to find a legitimate concern and take it over. There are strong indications that this is taking place in Lake County.'"*

If the Church was to support political social action of the kind Father Baroni and other Alinsky trained clerics envisioned, the Church needed to be restructured. To that end, they had convened the first Call to Action hearings and conference, orchestrating the process to appear as if there was widespread support for dissenting Catholic positions and community organizing.[37] Among many other things, Call to Action resolutions called for "a budgetary item of every parish

---

[32] *Geno*, p. 92.

[33] James B. Lane, Edward J. Escobar, *Forging a Community: The Latino Experience in Northwest Indiana, 1919-1975*(Indiana University Press: 1987), p. 254. The Industrial Areas Foundation's Chicago training is called in this book and elsewhere the Alinsky Institute.

[34] *Geno*, p. 94.

[35] Andrew Hurley, *Environmental Inequalities: Class, Race, and Industrial Pollution in Gary, Indiana, 1945-1980* (University of North Carolina Press, 1995), p. 106; 108.

[36] Father William Byron, S.J. "The Baroni Principles for Social Action," *Salt of the Earth*, Nov-Dec 1996.

[37] For a detailed history of the Call to Action hearings, conference, and position papers, see Stephanie Block, *Change Agents: Alinskyian Organizing Among Religious Bodies*, Volume I, chapter 2.

to support competent neighborhood/community action groups," diocesan resources "for training current and potential leaders" in community organizing, and diocesan funding to support "competent neighborhood/community action groups." [38]

Alinskyian organizing – not the Church or the school or any other institution – was seen as the structure by which urban life might be humanized. At a White House Conference on Ethnicity and Neighborhoods, Father Baroni complained that cities were no longer civilizing influences because of a breakdown of *civitas*:

Civitas was the religious and political association of families and tribes - the people bound together in civic association. ….Urban research and urban policy are bankrupt because of their lack of attention to the *civitas* — their lack of attention to *civic* renewal and *civic* development. By focusing on urban concerns, the physical items, to the exclusion of *civic* concerns, national urban policy has nearly destroyed *the civitas* — the various levels of human community which make urban life possible."[39]

To reclaim *civitas* was the work of community organizing, backed by religious institutions. In other words, one way to restore *civitas* was through faith-based organizing, Alinskyian organizing. "[U]rban policy must be rethought and refashioned into a *civic* policy — a policy which in broadest outline is cognizant of our *civic* life and supportive of the preeminent features of *civic* life which have been thoughtlessly squandered — our rich variety of religious and cultural associations which have been the sustaining structures of our urban neighborhoods."[40]

It was an interesting thesis for a priest.

To emphasize how thoroughly profane Father Baroni's vision had become, the O'Rourke biography provides a pivotal snapshot of the 1970s, struck by two Supreme Court decisions that legalized abortion during all nine months of a mother's pregnancy.

Father Baroni accepted Church teaching that abortion is a moral evil, "but was skeptical about accomplishing that through the legal and law enforcement systems." He preferred to focus on the business of revitalizing the *civitas* and rebuilding neighborhoods.

> *"But the Democrats pointed out to Baroni that unless they handled the abortion issue, they could not get elected, and that would doom many of the other programs in which Baroni had an interest. Baroni worked out an answer."*

---

[38] "A Call to Action: The Justice Conference Resolutions of the Church," *Origins,* November 4, 1976, Section on "Neighborhoods, Recommendation concerning "The Church and Neighborhood Action," # 2.
[39] Geno Baroni, "Neighborhood Revitalization: Neighborhood Policy for a Pluralistic Urban Society," in *Ethnicity and Neighborhood: Proceedings, Whitehouse Conference,* May 5, 1976, pp. 4-5.
[40] "Neighborhood Revitalization…"

"But the Democrats pointed out to Baroni that unless they handled the abortion issue, they could not get elected, and that would doom many of the other programs in which Baroni had an interest. Baroni worked out an answer."[41]

The answer was to decry single-issue politics, insist that the voter must consider the broad range of issues, and to advise candidates to "dwell on the economic bread and butter issues that had attracted Catholic middle and working class voters to the Democratic Party."[42]

This strategy has been operational ever since.

CCHD underwent several "reforms" over the years. The first was provoked by a 1997 Wanderer Forum Foundation Commentary that demonstrated CHD's Alinsky-style, church-based community organization grantees – particularly the ACORN network – were advancing highly politicized, and often left-wing, agendas. A copy was sent to every reigning bishop in the United States.

The result was a name change that added the word "Catholic" to the original "Campaign for Human Development and, by the summer of 1998, new guidelines had been issued emphasizing the sanctity of human life and clearly stating that not only must CHD funded *projects* conform to the moral teachings of the Catholic Church, but that any *organization* whose primary or substantial thrust was contrary to Catholic teaching – even if the project itself was in accord – would be denied funding.

But that's as far as it went. By 2005, grants for Alinskyian organizing had risen and funding for ACORN doubled, despite the fact that a good portion of the Commentary had concerned ACORN's progressive political activity – and numerous corruption charges against it.

CCHD paid dearly for that failure.

In the autumn of 2008, then-Senator Barack Obama was in the final lap of his run for president. His work as director of ACORN's partner organization, Project Vote, had become a matter of hot debate…particularly when it came out that Dale Rathke, the brother of ACORN founder Wade Rathke, had embezzled nearly $1 million from the organization between 1999 and 2000. The disclosure came on the heels of a slew of convictions, indictments, investigations, and lawsuits against ACORN for voter fraud…emphasizing not only the corruption but the naked political ambitions of the organization.

CCHD was in an embarrassing position. Over the 10 previous years, it had given more than $7.3 million to ACORN projects and $1.13 million just in 2008 alone. CCHD announced that it was suspending further funding to ACORN and, within a year, ACORN had folded, reorganizing under other names.

But CCHD soldiered on, insisting that the groups it funded were working on nonpartisan issues – and stoutly ignoring the progressive political activism of the remaining, still-funded Alinskyian organizations.

---

[41] *Geno,* p. 123.
[42] *Geno,* p. 130-1.

However, the pro-life community began to take notice. Always treated like a stepchild by the American Catholic bureaucracy, pro-life groups like the American Life League and Reform CCHD Now began their own analysis of CCHD grants, from the perspective of how they impacted life issues.

In 2011, they released a report exposing scores of grantees with direct ties to the promotion of abortion, as well as other problematic moral positions. CCHD acknowledged that five groups in the pro-life report "violated CCHD requirements" and pulled their funding while ignoring the much longer list of other grantees whose anti-Catholic actions were somehow acceptable.

That year, a "substantially revised CCHD Grant Agreement" was "used for all pending and future funding allocations and grants." That meant that groups, often run by non-Catholics but selected for CCHD grants, were asked to sign an agreement that they were in compliance with Catholic moral principles. Unfortunately, it didn't much affect CCHD funding patterns.

So in 2012, the pro-life community produced a second report, demonstrating that CCHD funding of progressive networks was pushing the "culture of death." In particular, they zeroed in on the Gamaliel Foundation Network, with over 50 U.S. affiliates[43] receiving $854,500 worth of CCHD grants the previous year. Gamaliel had been a founding member of the Fair Immigration Reform Movement (FIRM) Steering Committee, which in 2010 made an official position statement that homosexual relationships should be recognized as "families."

Again, CCHD did nothing…and continues to fund Gamaliel locals.

The pro-life report also looked at another Alinskyian organizing network, Interfaith Worker Justice, whose public policy and coalition-building has included support for same-sex "marriage," abortion, and democratic socialism among other things.

CCHD did nothing about that, either…and continues to fund Interfaith Worker Justice locals.

In fact, the percentage of CCHD grants to Alinskyian organizations continues to rise.

From its inception, CCHD set its goal on restructuring the U.S. according to a progressive political vision. Since then, it has primarily funded groups that network with progressive Democrats and/or democrat socialists.

For decades, the Alinskyians have burrowed inside of Catholic parishes, twisting Catholic social justice teaching to support compromising positions that advance a Culture of Death in a hundred, insidious ways.

---

[43] Lists of the (ever-changing) affiliates for each network can be found on each network website. These lists may not include affiliates that are in the early stages of organization.

The Evangelicals and the Baptists

In 1985, Rael Jean Isaac and Erich Isaac wrote a remarkable book called *The Coercive Utopians: Social Deception by America's Power Players*. It describes the movement of specific leftist political ideas throughout the various denominations of Christendom.

The Isaacs were careful to make the point that they are not chronicling a *conspiracy* but an *ideology* of people from "diverse backgrounds and traditions,"[45] who have concluded that capitalism is fundamentally flawed and are pursuing a common idealization of a perfected society based on restructured institutions.

The coercive utopians make no secret that their aim is power….the favorite method of the utopians, in staking out power, is to establish a community action organization. Typically, they consist of a small group of activists representing at most tiny minorities who claim to be representing majorities. Their techniques are based on the late Saul Alinsky, on whose book, *Rules for Radicals*, all community organizers base their campaigns.[46]

To accomplish the first step – power – the Alinskyian organizations rely heavily on government, church, and foundation funding.

Leftist theology has its roots in the "social gospel" spread among certain Protestant groups in the late nineteenth century.[47] "Social gospel" adherents believed that God expects human beings to create the "Kingdom of Heaven" by ridding the world of poverty, racism, and other social evils. The Rockefeller-funded Federal Council of Churches, the precursor of the National Council of Churches, formerly embraced the "social gospel" in 1908 and, during the Great Depression, these ideas spread rapidly through various US Protestant denominations.[48]

In the activist, anti-war years of the mid twentieth century, the "social gospel" branched in several directions. In Baptist and fundamentalist circles, its most lasting manifestation was in the 1973 formation of the **Evangelicals for Social Action** (ESA).[49] Its forty founding "evangelical

---

[44] More about this topic can be found in Stephanie Block's *Change Agents*, volume I.

[45] Rael Jean Isaac and Erich Isaac, *The Coercive Utopians: Social Deception by America's Power Players*, Discipleship Books (Regnery Gateway, Inc.), 1985, p 5.

[46] *The Coercive Utopians…*p 166, 167-168.

[47] The "social gospel" was a development of the ideas of Baptist minister Walter Rauschenbusch, who worked among the poor of New York City. "Unlike nineteenth-century reformers who sought to help the poor by teaching them the bourgeois virtues of hard work, thrift, and diligence, Rauschenbusch believed that the best way to uplift the downtrodden was to redistribute society's wealth and forge an egalitarian society. In Christ's name, capitalism had to fall. 'The Kingdom of God is a collective conception,' Rauschenbusch wrote in *Christianity and the Social Crisis*, politicizing the Gospel's message. 'It is not a matter of getting individuals to heaven, but of transforming the life on earth into the harmony of heaven.'" Steven Malanga, "The Religious Left, Reborn," *City Journal*, Autumn 2007.

[48] *The Coercive Utopians…*p 35.

[49] Evangelicals for Social Action website, About Us section, www.esa-online.org

leaders" issued the "Chicago Declaration of Evangelical Social Concern," arguing that the United States was beset with numerous evils:

…the materialism of our culture and the maldistribution of the nation's wealth and services…. the misplaced trust of the nation in economic and military might - a proud trust that promotes a national pathology of war and violence which victimizes our neighbors at home and abroad.….[and the encouragement of] men to prideful domination and women to irresponsible passivity.[50]

Rev. Jim Wallis was on the planning committee from which the ESA sprang.[51] Wallis is a writer and a progressive political activist who founded and edits *Sojourners* magazine and directs an organization by the same name. He is the non-denomination Evangelical Protestant minister who gave the dedication prayer for Democrat President Barack Obama's second inauguration.

In 1983, Sojourners co-created Witness for Peace Tours to generate pro-Sandinista (Marxist) support in the United States. United States delegates were taken to Nicaragua and treated to staged "pep rallies," supposedly demonstrating popular enthusiasm for the Sandinistas.[52]

Meanwhile, back home, *Sojourners* magazine wrote glowing articles about liberation theology's inroads into the spiritual life of Latin Americans,[53] portrayed the US military and US Latin American foreign policy as "anti-Christ,"[54] and claimed that US economic assistance went exclusively to countries that repress and torture their citizens.[55]

So Sojourners has always been interested in left-wing political causes. In anticipation of the 1996 elections, Wallis convened what was, at the time, called an "evangelical para-church political action group," Call to Renewal – Christians for a New Political Vision, "created out of the perceived need to present an alternative viewpoint to the dominant conservative political agenda – represented by such groups as the boards of Christian Coalition."[56] At one point, its literature described Call to Renewal as "an interfaith effort to end poverty" and during the summer of 2006 it merged boards with Sojourners.[57]

---

[50] Evangelicals for Social Action, "Chicago Declaration of Evangelical Social Concern," November 25, 1973, Chicago, Illinois

[51] Billy Graham Center, Archives, "Evangelicals for Social Action - Collection 37," www.wheaton.edu/bgc/archives/GUIDES/037.htm

[52] Edmund W. Robb and Julia Robb, *The Betrayal of the Church*, Crossway Books, 1986; Witness for Peace, Mission and History page, www.witnessforpeace.org.

[53] Joan Harris, *The Sojourners File*, New Century Foundation, 1983, pp 4-5.

[54] *The Sojourners File*…p 8-9, quoting *Sojourners*, July/August 1981, p 7.

[55] *The Sojourners File*…p 23-24, quoting *Sojourners*, June 1977, pp 3-4.

[56] University of Virginia, New Religious Movements: Call to Renewal - Christians for a New Political Vision, web.archive.org/web/20060830125446/religiousmovements.lib.virginia.edu/nrms/Callrenu.html

[57] Sojourners, About Us, "The reunification of Sojourners and Call to Renewal," www.sojo.net/index.cfm?action=about_us.reunification

Call to Renewal partners and affiliates were a modest fellowship, comprised primarily of progressive protestant organizations and a handful of powerful Catholic groups.[58] In some instances, it described itself as politically "moderate"[59] though that was hardly the case as its efforts were entirely directed toward putting progressive candidates in office.

In the face of the 2008 presidential elections, under the auspices of the Center for American Progress, Wallis and other progressive "faith leaders" began a more ambitious – and much more sophisticated –project, Faith in Public Life. The website for Faith in Public Life at that time explained that its founding was sparked by the 2004 elections to support what it called the "social justice faith movement" and develop "increased and effective collaboration, coordination, and communication on the national, state and local level." In contrast to the "religious right," Faith in Public Life eschewed, according to its spokes-folk at the time, the issues of abortion and homosexuality to focus on "social and economic justice" – although many of its associate groups argue that abortion and homosexual rights *are* social and economic justice issues.[60]

"Social gospel" theology has also spawned support of community organizing through **Christians Supporting Community Organizing** (CSCO), founded in 1997[61] by progressively-minded Evangelicals, Pentecostals, Baptists, and other "related Christian leaders." In explaining their work in this capacity, CSCO writes, "We are persuaded that local congregations of our faith perspectives should explore congregation-based community organizing as a means to faithfully live out the Gospel."[62]

Bob Linthicum, a CSCO "leader," created and directed World Vision International's[63] Office of Urban Advance" for community organizing in 1985. [64] He prepared a training curriculum, "Biblical Foundations for Community Organizing." "Interest in the Project's theological work led IAF to contract with Linthicum to help train IAF leaders and organizers throughout northern California, Oregon and Washington. PICO organizers have enrolled in Project-sponsored workshops."[65]

Organizing among Presbyterians and Lutherans

---

[58] Call to Renewal Network, Listing of Partners, Affiliates, and Collaborating Organizations: www.calltorenewal.com/network.cfm (accessed 10-7-01)

[59] Mark Tooley, "Sojourn to the Center: Has Religious-Left Activist Jim Wallis Gone Moderate?" *Touchstone Magazine*, April 2002.

[60] Chapter 34 discusses Faith in Public Life in more detail.

[61] 1997 is the founding date given at the CSCO website: www.cscoweb.org/brief.html; however, the CSCO member profile on the Colorado Association of Nonprofit Organizations website from 2001 says CSCO was founded/incorporated in 1994.

[62] Christians Supporting Community Organizing website, "Proclamation and Call to Our Churches, Preamble," www.cscoweb.org/proc.html

[63] World Vision International is an Evangelical organization to provide aid and advocacy around the world.

[64] Robert Linthicum, "Doing Community Organizing in the Urban Slums of India," Social Policy, 12-22-01; Dr Robert Linthicum official website: www.rclinthicum@org

[65] David Scheie, with T Williams and Luisa Pessoa-Brandão, Organized Religion and Civic Culture: Final Report from a Strategic Review," prepared for The James Irvine Foundation, April 2001. (3/99 report, p.3, 3/98 report attachment, Craig McGarvey comment in 1/01)

The "social gospel" is alive and kicking among the mainstream Protestant denominations, as well. A recent example of this thought is echoed in a quote from Bishop Roy Dixon, prelate of the Southern California 4th ecclesiastical jurisdiction of the Church of God in Christ, a member of the San Diego Organizing Project, and former board chair of the PICO National Network (of which SDOP is an affiliate). Defending the work of community organizers, Dixon said, "When people come together in my church hall to improve our community, they're building the Kingdom of God in San Diego. We see the fruits of community organizing in safer streets, new parks, and new affordable housing."

There's a price to be paid for this new "gospel," however. Every denomination in which it has taken root, has experienced a rift. The US Presbyterian Church, for example, is divided between the PCUSA – the Presbyterian Church in the United States of America – and more theologically conservative branches of the denomination.

In 2005, the PCUSA signed a joint statement with the Evangelical Lutheran Church of America to become more involved nationally with community organizing. It's a fascinating position paper, the product of a national gathering coordinated by the Urban Ministry Office of the Presbyterian Church (USA) and the Congregation-based Community Organizing/Leadership Development for Public Life Office of the Evangelical Lutheran Church in America.[66] It observes that congregation-based (faith-based) community organizing, already an established fact in many congregations, has "proven to be a revitalizing strategy for congregations and expands the reach and vision of ministry." It therefore advocates that each denomination increase funding for organizing and explore the ways it "can be a vital part of congregational re-development and new church development…. working together with other denominations on a national strategy around public policy using a community organizing framework."

For seminarians, there is the particular recommendation to "engage in appropriate learning projects related to congregation-based community organizing. Faculties of seminaries [should] be encouraged to provide resources to the larger church of the theological and biblical foundations of social justice through a CBCO [congregation-based community organizing] strategy."

Congregations are mandated to employ "the strategies of community organizing – individual meetings, house meetings, building a relational culture – for congregational transformation….[u]sing CBCO as a primary strategy for mission, understanding its systemic approach as compared to direct service or advocacy."

For its part, the liberal Evangelical Lutheran Church in America (ELCA) was born in 1987, the product of various splits and realignments among the US Lutheran population.[67] Almost immediately after its inception, the ELCA began meeting with members of the larger, national organizing networks. From these discussions, the ELCA developed a six-point strategic plan on

---

[66] "Lutheran—Presbyterian Congregation-based Community Organizing Consultation," signed October 13-15, 2005, www.interfaithfunders.org/PresbandLutherans.html. Following several quotes are from this source.

[67] www.elca.org carries a detailed history

the integration of faith-based organizing throughout the denomination, hoping "to produce a powerful force that can act as a real agent of social change."[68]

The four major Alinskyian networks are all involved in the project – the IAF, DART, Gamaliel, and PICO – and openly state that the "ultimate goal of this effort is to change the culture of the church so that community organizing is an integral part of every congregation of the ELCA."[69]

So while the ELCA is moving toward the goal of reinventing itself as an earthly "agent of social change," the denomination has been changing doctrinally, too. Official positions on homosexuality – expressing the traditional, Biblical belief that marriage is between a man and woman, that homosexual erotic activity is sinful, and that people leading homosexually active lives cannot hold positions of ministry – have been shifting over the last two decades. Naturally, the newly organized ELCA will bring its new moral values into the public – and political –arena.

> *The four major Alinskyian networks are all involved in the [strategic plan to integrate faith-based organizing throughout the ECLA] – the IAF, DART, Gamaliel, and PICO – and openly state that the "ultimate goal of this effort is to change the culture of the church so that community organizing is an integral part of every congregation of the ELCA."*

United Methodists

The United Methodists have had a particularly interesting relationship to Alinskyian organizing. Despite decades of support for extraordinarily left-wing causes,[70] there was division within the denomination over it. The now defunct Alinskyian organization, the Rural Organizing Committee (ROC) in Holmes County, Mississippi, "received core funding from the United Methodist Church for almost ten years." Comprised predominantly of "blacks," ROC was extremely successful in getting "black people into many elected and bureaucratic positions." As a result, they began to:

…threaten the white power elite. Most of the elite were Methodists. Last year [late 1980s] the Methodist Church cut off funding to ROC and they have to lay off their full-time staff. Although some of them are continuing to work without money, they believe the whole project is in serious jeopardy. They had not foreseen this coming, even when

---

[68] www.faithinpubliclife.org/content/case-studies/partnerships_between_national.html; The ELCA has a website for those interested in its organizing efforts: www.elca.org/Our-Faith-In-Action/Justice/Congregation-based-Organizing.aspx or www2.elca.org/organizing/about
[69] www.faithinpubliclife.org/content/case-studies/partnerships_between_national.html
[70] An examination of the United Methodist's funding of radical left-wing groups, its exposure in the late 1970s by David Jessup, and subsequent actions to address the criticism raised can be read in *The Coercive Utopians.*

the United Methodists began to fire all national staff that supported community organizing work.[71]

United Methodist support for the Alinskyian networks, however, wasn't inconsequential. For a number of years, Industrial Areas Foundation Regional Trainings have been held at the Drew University Theological School – "a theology school with Methodist roots and ecumenical concerns."[72] Drew seminarians have the fee waived if they attend the 5-day IAF training.[73]

> *Drew seminarians have the fee waived if they attend the 5-day IAF training.*

At least one United Methodist bishop has had a rather substantial career in Alinskyian faith-based organizing. Since the 1980s, Minerva Carcaño, now Bishop of the Phoenix Episcopal Area of the United Methodist Southwest Conference, has been actively engaged with "community organizing ministry through the Industrial Areas Foundation."[74]

Some modest United Methodist grants are awarded to network affiliates. For example, a local "Justice Education and Leadership Development Program (JEALD)" was awarded $12,000 for "a congregational effort to engage young adults in community organizing efforts through two Gamaliel Foundation organizing workshops, as well as restorative justice training. JEALD will address domestic violence prevention and juvenile offender ministries. The grant will be used to train five persons and provide peace with justice materials."[75] It's neither an enormous sum nor a large project but, over time, such investments yield dividends.

Union for Reform Judaism

The Jewish funding mechanism for Alinskyian organizing – **Jewish Funds for Justice** (JFSJ) – describes itself as a national public foundation "to combat the root causes of domestic social and economic injustice." To accomplish that, the JFSJ began a "national initiative" in 2002, to support congregation-based community organizing.

Our goal was to address the lack of sustained engagement in activities beyond direct service programs and to challenge congregations to address systemic issues relating to domestic poverty and social injustice," the JFSJ website explains. Congregation-based community organizing "unites a diverse range of people, primarily through religious congregations, in the shared goal of building a civic power base capable of making

---

[71] Joan Newman Kuyek, *Fighting for Hope: Organizing to Realize Our Dreams*, Black Rose Books, 1990, p 166
[72] www.drew.edu/history.aspx
[73] www.drew.edu/theo/cue.aspx?id=6007
[74] Virginia Armstrong, "Methodist Church Members Ask to Quit Valley Interfaith, Valley Morning Star, 10-28-84. The article describes Carcaño's church, El Divino Redentor Methodist of McAllen, Texas petitioning to withdraw from affiliation with the IAF-affiliate Valley Interfaith; Minerva G. Carcaño, Wikipedia entry
[75] United Methodist General Board of Church and Society, "United Methodist social justice agency awards $155,000 in Ethnic Local Church funding," 11-3-08.

change to promote the public good. Today, nearly 100 synagogues across the United States are engaged in or actively exploring CBCO.[76]

"Congregation-based community organizing" means something very specific to the JFSJ, namely membership in one of four Alinskyian organizing networks. In 2008, that's where JFSJ awarded a healthy percentage of its grants.

Rabbi Jonah Pesner serves on JFSJ's Jewish Clergy Task Force.[77] He's also co-chair of the Boston Industrial Areas Foundation affiliate and also is the founding director of **Just Congregations,** a social action program developed by the Union of Reform Judaism and the JFSJ in 2006 to train Jewish congregations across the country in IAF-based organizing. Just Congregations provides the "language and organizing out of their faith tradition," since "the language of Christianity, in particular, can make Jews uncomfortable and hesitant to participate. Exacerbating these feelings can be conflicting positions by the two faiths on issues such as abortion and gay rights."[78]

In addition to grants, Just Congregations and the JFSJ – which trains rabbinic and cantorial students in synagogue organizing through its Leadership for Public Life program – provide numerous resources supportive of Alinskyian organizing. According to Just Congregations literature, they recruit synagogue leaders for the national gathering, engage clergy in congregation-based community organizing task forces, connect leaders locally to JFSJ initiatives, and encourage seminary faculty and students to support and attend CBCO seminary training sessions. "[M]ost importantly, the Union/Just Congregations staff members would coordinate a national strategy together with JFSJ staff to determine together which geographic regions are ripe to be targeted for Reform Jewish engagement in CBCO."[79]

Unitarian Universalists

The Unitarian Universalist Association of Congregations (UUA or UU) is also on the congregation-based, community organizing bandwagon and published "Congregation-Based Community Organizing: A Social Justice Approach to Revitalizing Congregational Life" in 2006.

This guide begins with a theological grounding for CBCO in pursuit of social justice and analyzes what prevents many contemporary Unitarian Universalists from being more assertively engaged. The guide then describes how CBCO builds community, makes concrete changes to promote the public good, and develops community leaders. It

---

[76] Jewish Funds for Justice website, "Congregation Based Community Organizing," www.jewishjustice.org/jfsj.php?page=2.5
[77] Before the 2008 presidential elections in the United States, Rabbi Jonah Presner was also a spokesman for *Faith in Public Life*, an organization that targets religious bodies with progressive political messages.
[78] Daniel Levisohn, Assistant Editor, JTNews: "Faith Alliance reaches out to Jewish congregations," www.jtnews.net/index.php?/news/item/899
[79] urj.org/justcongregations/jfsj

describes the benefits reaped by participating congregations, including the building of interfaith, interclass, and interracial relationships; the addition of new congregational members; the development of leaders; and the new dynamism that transforms congregational life. The guide also analyzes the challenges to congregational participation in CBCO and the ways in which congregations can meet those challenges.[80]

The UUA guide also speaks of "shifting the paradigm." Its sense of "social justice" includes work, in its own words "for civil and human rights; for rights for gay men, lesbians, bisexuals, and transgendered people; for a healthier environment; for economic justice; and for peace and world community."[81] The tool for attaining long-term, "social justice" change is, of course, congregation-based community organization, and the guide mentions the major Alinskyian organizing networks, concluding:

> *The Unitarian Universalist Funding Program provides grants to ...."nonprofit organizations addressing issues of social and economic justice. Grants are given to projects that use community organizing to bring about systemic change."*

Congregation-based community organizing is an effective way to fulfill our mandate to work for a better world fully consistent with UU values, principles, and theology. Part of the mission of UU congregations is to move outside our walls and join in building bridges across the barriers that separate people from one another. It is the work of restoring, creating, and maintaining right relationships. Over a hundred of our fellowships and churches are engaged with local network affiliates, where they build multiclass, multirace, and multifaith organizations through grass-roots organizing. At the Unitarian Universalist Association, we wish to encourage and expand congregational participation in this movement. [82]

The Unitarian Universalist Funding Program provides grants to community organizing through funds provided by the **Unitarian Universalist Veatch Program at Shelter Rock**. Specifically, its **Fund for UU Social Responsibility** "makes grants to projects that increase UU involvement in social responsibility," including a matching grants program for Congregation-Based Community Organizing and the **Fund for a Just Society**, which "makes grants to nonprofit organizations addressing issues of social and economic justice. Grants are given to projects that use community organizing to bring about systemic change."[83]

---

[80] www.uua.org/leaders/justice/cbco/27243.shtml
[81] Unitarian Universalist Association of Congregations, "Congregation-Based Community Organizing: A Social Justice Approach to Revitalizing Congregational Life," 2006.
[82] "Congregation-Based Community Organizing..."
[83] Unitarlian Universalist Association of Congregations, "The Unitarian Universalist Funding Program," undated, www.uua.org/giving/fundingprogram

Interfaith Funders and the Inter-Religious Organizing Initiative

Just as embracing the "social gospel" has led to internal denominational splits, it has created new alliances of people across denominational lines. Interfaith Funders (IF) is one such alliance – a "network of faith-based and secular grantmakers committed to social change and economic justice," but most specifically "to advance the field of congregation-based community organizing (CBCO, also known as Faith-based Community Organizing, FBCO)." [84]

Groups that have become members of Interfaith Funders are those that are most invested in congregation-based – Alinskyian – community organizing. [85] In addition to their own funding mechanisms, they are able to award "collaborative grants" through Interfaith Funders. Some of these grants go towards research projects supportive of congregation-based community organizing and to "provide workshops on CBCO at funder conferences and briefings, and gatherings of faith communities, as well as individual meetings. IF also offers members valuable networking and internal education." [86]

To facilitate networking among organizers, Interfaith Funders launched the **Inter-Religious Organizing Initiative** (IOI) in 2002, when ELCA Presiding Bishop Mark Hanson and Dr. William Shaw, President of the National Baptist Convention USA "convened a meeting of their peers from several national faith bodies. They discussed cooperative civic action according to the principles of congregation-based organizing. The result was the commissioning of the "IOI Table." [87] Faith leaders at "the Table" commit to involving their congregations more deeply in public life and to developing national power building processes. [88]

The IOI Table includes not only Interfaith Funders' members but also representatives from the primary Alinskyian organizing networks, as well as Faith in Public Life. [89]

Specific "justice issues" are selected as appropriate for engagement at the national level – issues selected from among "those which arise out of the grassroots organizing efforts of participating networks, which converge with the interests of participating denominations and religious bodies…," drawing on "media and communications consultants, theologians, denominational advocacy offices, political analysts, and experts in message framing" to shape

---

[84] www.interfaithfunders.org/aboutus.html

[85] As of August 2010, there were 12 members: The Evangelical Lutheran Church In America's Division for Church in Society, One Great Hour of Sharing Fund of the Presbyterian Church (U.S.A.), Catholic Campaign for Human Development, Unitarian Universalist Veatch Program at Shelter Rock, Jewish Funds for Justice, The McKnight Foundation, The Nathan Cummings Foundation, Dominican Sisters of Springfield, Missionary Oblates of Mary Immaculate, C.S. Mott Foundation, The Needmor Fund, Linchpin Project of the Center for Community Change, and Unitarian Universalist Funding Panels. www.interfaithfunders.org/aboutus.html

[86] www.interfaithfunders.org/aboutus.html

[87] www.elca.org/Our-Faith-In-Action/Justice/Congregation-based-Organizing/Enewsletter.aspx#4

[88] Inter-Religious Organizing Initiative (IOI) Working Table, "A Statement of the IOI Planning Team," revised August 1, 2007. The Planning Team members included: Terry Boggs, ELCA; Dennis Jacobsen, ELCA; Charles Mock, National Baptist Convention, USA, Inc.; Cris Doby, Charles Stewart Mott Foundation; Len Dubi, Archdiocese of Chicago; and Kathy Partridge, Interfaith Funders.

[89] "UUA Joins Interfaith Organizing Initiative at Historic Gathering in Nashville," News, 12-19-07; "A Statement of the IOI Planning Team…" also mentions The Center for Community Change (CCC).

"its public voice and national strategy."[90]

Secular Funders

The above has focused on the funding provided by religious bodies to promote the faith-based, Alinskyian organizing networks. Secular bodies are deeply invested in them, as well.

Page 14 of the 2009 Annual Report for the Gamaliel Foundation lists its organizational contributors.[91] Some of them are what one would expect, such as the Presbyterian Church USA (in other words, religious bodies) and the Ford and Rockefeller Foundations who have been funding faith-based organizing for years.[92]

Others are less expected – for example, the Service Employees International Union (SEIU). Faith in Public Life is another curious contributor. This organization describes itself as a "strategy center advancing faith in the public square as a positive and unifying force for justice, compassion and the common good."[93] Funding an Alinskyian organizing network, in other words, is a Faith in Public Life strategy to advance its vision of justice.   The contribution to Gamaliel's work "buys" a stake in Gamaliel's efforts among faith institutions to spread the "vision" – which defines "justice" in progressive, political terms.

Another particularly interesting contributor to the Gamaliel Foundation is the Center for Community Change (CCC), which was created to provide technical assistance to various local community organizations. Under the leadership of former ACORN organizer Deepak Bhargava, it has become a "political machine," coordinating local organizations such as Gamaliel affiliates, which are CCC "partners," in national campaigns.

The next question is where do Faith in Public Life and the Center for Community Change get the money to give to Gamaliel? Among *their* contributors is George Soros' Open Society Institute.[94]

George Soros' Open Society Institute's funding of Gamaliel – or in, for that matter, Faith in Public Life, CCC, and the other Alinskyian organizing networks [95] – is an investment in progressive values.   Open Society Institute has also generously funded:
  · Catholics for a Free Choice,

---

[90] "A Statement of the IOI Planning Team…"
[91] www.gamaliel.org/Portals/0/Documents/Gamaliel2009AnnualReport.pdf
[92] *The Coercive Utopians* (1985) details this funding source.
[93] faithinpubliclife.org/about
[94] All Open Society Institute grants cited here can be found at the OSI website, grantee listings:
www.soros.org/initiatives/usprograms/focus/democracy/grants/civic/grantees?sort_on=sort_title&sort_desc=0&start:int=0
[95] Open Society Institute funded the Industrial Areas Foundation network through its "organizing, technical assistance, training, and research" component, the Interfaith Education Fund, which received an 18-month grant for $300,000 in 2008 and another 1-year grant for $200,000 in 2010. The PICO network received a 2-year Open Society Institute grant for $600,000 in 2009. National Training and Information Center received a 2009 Open Society Institute grant for $600,000 over a 2-year period. Catholics in Alliance for the Common Good (the now defunct twin of Faith in Public Life's Catholics United) received $50,000 in 2005, $100,000 in 2006, and another $100,000 in 2009 from the Open Society Institute. [See *Anne Hendershott, "Who are these Fake Catholic Groups," The Catholic Advocate, 3-18-10]*

- Planned Parenthood,
- National Abortion Rights Action League (NARAL), and
- a host of other abortion "rights" organizations.

Just as egregiously, it has funded the United Religions Initiative (URI), which promulgates the idea that all religions and spiritual movements are equally "true" and with it the concept that the goal of the spiritual is social reform – including the principle of population control.[96] The faith-based Alinskyian organizing networks are right there, working "for change" among Catholics and Evangelicals and other religious bodies that might, historically, have been expected to resist progressive positions such as these.

Alinsky and the organizers he trained have been highly successful in raising money from religious institutions for their "people's organizations" but it has cost these institutions a good deal more than dues and grants. They have paid for their cooperation in secular political activism with a profound distortion of their faith. In exchange, even by secular standards, they've received nothing in return – according to the United States Census Bureau, in 1960 around 12 percent of Americans lived in poverty. By 2013, the number had risen to about 14.5 percent.[97]

Perhaps it's time to try implementing *authentic* social justice.

---

[96] See Lee Penn, *False Dawn: The United Religions Initiative, Globalism, and the Quest for a One-World Religion*, Sophia Perennis, 2004.
[97] US Census Bureau, Table 9: Poverty, by Region, www.census.gov/hhes/www/poverty/data/historical/people.html

The thoughts of Lord Jonathan Sacks, chief rabbi of the United Hebrew Congregations of the Commonwealth, are often quoted by the Alinskyian community organizing affiliates of Great Britain. In a 2011 editorial, Lord Sacks wrote:

> [T]his was no political uprising. People were breaking into shops and making off with clothes, shoes, electronic gadgets and flat-screen televisions. It was, as someone later called it, shopping with violence, consumerism run rampage, an explosion of lawlessness made possible by mobile phones as gangs discovered that by text messaging they could bring crowds onto the streets where they became, for a while, impossible to control.[98]

What brought on this orgy of anarchy? Rabbi Sacks believes that the moral revolution of the 1960s, with its abandonment of the "traditional ethic of self-restraint," particularly sex without the responsibility of marriage, spawned a generation of troubled children. Many of the rioting youth belong to a demographic of uninvolved fathers and overworked, unmarried mothers. Gangs fill up the vacuum of an absent family and bring with them drugs, crime, and violence.

> The truth is, it is not their fault. They are the victims of the tsunami of wishful thinking that washed across the West saying that you can have children without the responsibility of parenthood, social order without the responsibility of citizenship, liberty without the responsibility of morality and self-esteem without the responsibility of work and earned achievement.

This is all true. Children need to be raised, not merely spawned; a community needs enfranchised citizens:

> There are large parts of Britain, Europe and even the United States where religion is a thing of the past and there is no counter-voice to the culture of buy it, spend it, wear it, flaunt it, because you're worth it. The message is that morality is passé, conscience is for wimps, and the single overriding command is "Thou shalt not be found out."

Religious institutions once instilled good citizenship into society. They fostered the values of "moral character, self-discipline, willpower and personal responsibility." So, for example, Alexis de Tocqueville, visiting the United States in 1831, found:

> … a secular state, to be sure, but also a society in which religion was, he said, the first of its political (we would now say "civil") institutions. It did three things he saw as

---

[98] "Reversing the Decay of London Undone: Britain's chief rabbi on the moral disintegration since the 1960s and how to rebuild," *Wall Street Journal*, August 20, 2011.

essential. It strengthened the family. It taught morality. And it encouraged active citizenship.

This is where it begins to get problematic. "Religious people... make better neighbors and citizens," Rabbi Sacks continues, quoting a contemporary author, Robert Putnam. Society "needs religion: not as doctrine but as a shaper of behavior, a tutor in morality, an ongoing seminar in self-restraint and pursuit of the common good."

Rabbi Sacks closes with a particularly informative story:

> One of our great British exports to America, Harvard historian Niall Ferguson, has a fascinating passage in his recent book "Civilization," in which he asks whether the West can maintain its primacy on the world stage or if it is a civilization in decline.[99]
>
> He quotes a member of the Chinese Academy of Social Sciences, tasked with finding out what gave the West its dominance. He said: At first we thought it was your guns. Then we thought it was your political system, democracy. Then we said it was your economic system, capitalism. But for the last 20 years, we have known that it was your religion.
>
> It was the Judeo-Christian heritage that gave the West its restless pursuit of a tomorrow that would be better than today. The Chinese have learned the lesson. Fifty years after Chairman Mao declared China a religion-free zone, there are now more Chinese Christians than there are members of the Communist Party.

[A] member of the Chinese Academy of Social Sciences, tasked with finding out what gave the West its dominance...said: "At first we thought it was your guns. Then we thought it was your political system, democracy. Then we said it was your economic system, capitalism. But for the last 20 years, we have known that it was your religion."

No one is arguing the verity of this analysis. But it leads the Alinskyites, as it led the Communist Chinese, to put religion at the service of society. A well-oiled society is the goal; organized religions – religious institutions – are a *means*.

Marx said "religion is the opium of the people," meaning that it took people's attention from the work of creating a just society and focused it on pie-in-the-sky hopes. It dulled the pain of life on earth without addressing the root causes of that pain.

---

[99] Jonathan Sacks, "Reversing the Decay of London Undone: Britain's chief rabbi on the moral disintegration since the 1960s and how to rebuild," editorial,
By
August 20, 2011

The Alinskyites and the Chinese Communists have turned this around. The opium of religion makes people better workers and better socialized. Give them their opium, then, but harness it. Keep attention focused on the earth.

The trouble with this way of thinking is that it kills the golden goose. True religion – religion for the sake of drawing Man closer to the Divine – *does* produce secondary benefits that serve society but religion for the sake of society isn't authentic and will quickly lose its appeal. To the degree that secular organizations or the State tamper with religious institutions, attempting to direct their energies (more government money to Catholic Charities, say), is the degree to which those institutions become less effective at building good citizens.

> *The opium of religion makes people better workers and better socialized. Give them their opium, then, but harness it. Keep attention focused on the earth.*

One of the Gamaliel networks' efforts has been to foster a "clergy caucus," a group of religious leaders who can provide (in Alinskyian terms) the moral – or, even better, the *theological*—garment in which its issues may most profitably be cloaked. *Theological*, in this context, means giving the issue a spin that will be persuasive to people who operate within a particular religious framework.

For example, in Gamaliel's Literature Library,[100] one can download a Gamaliel National Clergy Caucus "Theological Statement" titled "Civil Rights for All Immigrants."[101]

The statement opens with a number of scripture passages exhorting the believer, Jewish and Christian, to "welcome the stranger." It develops this line of thinking by saying that:

> [T]he biblical tradition reveals God as present in the strangers welcomed by Abraham and Sarah (Genesis 18), as the liberator of the Chosen People from their forced sojourn and enslavement in the land of Egypt, and ....that Jesus was a refugee in Egypt (Matthew 2) and is encountered in the experience of strangers, refugees, and migrants throughout history (Matthew 25:38); and that as people of God we are part of a world-wide community, which extends beyond exclusionary borders and which embraces refugees and immigrants. ...all human beings are created in the image of God and therefore enjoy an innate human dignity with the right to food, shelter, freedom and the opportunity to provide for their own good and the good of society.

From this "theological" basis, the statement continues to say that in situations where individuals feel they "must migrate in order to support and protect" themselves, "nation*s who are able to receive them should do so whenever possible.*" The italics are in the original and indicate

---

[100] www.gamaliel.org/Literaturelibrary.aspx
[101] GNCCtheologicalStatementWashingtonFinal.pdf

a thought lifted from "Strangers No Longer: Together on the Journey of Hope: A Pastoral Letter Concerning Migration from the Catholic Bishops of Mexico and the United States" which, in fairness, is a good deal more complex than this text-proving by Gamaliel would lead one to think.

Of course, what's missing is the acknowledgment that it is the *nation* that must decide whether it can receive these needy strangers, and under what conditions, and in what numbers. Gamaliel, by virtue of its organizing the people who have come illegally to the US to fight for their "right" to be here – which Gamaliel has done – has placed that determination with the strangers themselves. The Gamaliel theologians, even while recognizing the generosity of the United States towards immigrants, are not *exhorting* the United States to greater generosity but are *demanding* it. They are not urging the thoughtful assimilation of needy individuals but are insisting on a porous, largely unregulated border – based on a fabricated Biblical mandate for it.

Gamaliel also calls for a full spectrum of civil "rights" that include the absolutely *reasonable* and ethical expectation that all people, regardless of citizenship, must be granted protection of their fundamental civil liberties and the absolutely *unreasonable* expectation that no one is to be threatened with deportation for "minor offenses." May a sovereign state make no distinctions among the "strangers" who enter its lands? No matter how one toys with the scriptures, that isn't what they say.

By all means, wealthier countries can and ought to have a discussion about what constitutes "humane border enforcement policies that, while protecting the security of this nation, emphasize the safety and dignity of immigrants and offer a legal, safe, and orderly alternative for those seeking to cross our borders in order to work."[102] That's a good and important discussion for a nation to have.

However, there are *two* positions that have moral content. One is the treatment of people who have entered the country illegally – about which the Gamaliel theological statement has a great many things to say. The other is the obligation of a State to protect its citizens – about which the Gamaliel theological statement has nothing to say beyond recognizing that it exists. The Gamaliel theologians have *used* theological considerations to bolster the part of the argument that interested them and ignored any further theological considerations that temper the "rights" of the stranger with the "rights" of the citizen…or, to express it more appropriately, that would have clarified the responsibilities of both.

Propaganda written to sound "theological" isn't real theology.

Alinskyian community organizations frequently pull bits of Scripture or Catholic social teaching from Church documents and, using them out of context, proof- text[103] fallacious positions. It may be well-intentioned but the problem is serious for the Church that is already bleeding in multiple directions because its people are, in the words of the late Cardinal Bernadin,

---

[102] "Civil Rights for All Immigrants: A Statement of the Gamaliel Foundation and Religious Leaders," undated: www.gamaliel.org/Portals/0/Documents/GNCCtheologicalStatementFinal8.5x11.pdf

[103] Proof-texting is the (mis)use of a Bible verse, taken out of context, to justify a position that the scripture doesn't hold.

largely religious illiterates.[104]   Allowing false teachers access to an ignorant, vulnerable flock is tantamount to evangelizing them right out of their faith.

Liberationism is a serious distortion of not only Catholic social teaching but of its doctrinal teachings, as well. Before his election to the papacy, Benedict XVI prepared a Vatican response to the errors being spread by this theological movement, calling it "a perversion of the Christian message as God entrusted it to His Church." [105]

The issues provoking liberationism are genuine. On the other hand, some remedies may be as bad as the evils they seek to correct and their understanding of "justice" – the professed goal of liberationism – suffers from Marxist roots. They preach moral relativism, reduce spiritual pursuits to mere politics, and refuse to tackle the injustice of abortion because it's "too controversial."

> *This inclination to politicize the spiritual causes the liberationist to undervalue the effects of personal sin and overvalue structural (or societal) sin.*

This inclination to politicize the spiritual causes the liberationist to undervalue the effects of personal sin and overvalue structural (or societal) sin. As a result, economic or socio-political structures are misunderstood as root causes of evil rather than as a *consequence* of human actions, done by free and responsible persons. The Vatican document argues: "To demand first of all a radical revolution in social relations and then criticize the search for personal perfection is to set out on a road which leads to the denial of the meaning of the person and his transcendence, and to destroy ethics and its foundation which is the absolute character of the distinction between good and evil." [106]

The Instruction also notes that the radical deliverance of Christ, offered to both freeman and slave, "does not require some change in the political or social condition as a prerequisite for entrance into this freedom." [107] The Good News cannot be reduced to an earthly gospel, however.[108] Nor can scripture be used to teach that a given political or economic system liberates when "God is the defender and liberator of the poor." [109]

So we find, for example, in a booklet dedicated to the **Industrial Areas Foundation** for its work of identifying "groups of sinners as oppressed members of society who are marginalized and dehumanized by thoughtless oppressors" a "version" of the Magnificat[110] written by a group of IAF leaders, specifically, leaders from the San Antonio IAF local, Communities Organized for Public Service (COPS). This reformulation of scripture is offered as an example of how one is "to reflect on the Gospels in order to find the proper response to our own situation" when using a see-judge-act pedagogy of conscientization.

---

[104] Joseph Cardinal Bernardin, "Called to be Catholic: Church in a time of peril," August 12, 1996.
[105] Sacred Congregation for the Doctrine of the Faith, *Instruction on Certain Aspects of the "Theology of Liberation,"* 1984, IX.1.
[106] *Instruction...*IV.15
[107] *Instruction...* IV.13
[108] *Instruction...*VI.4
[109] *Instruction...*IV.6
[110] Luke 1:46-55

C.O.P.S. Manifesto
Communities Organized for Public Service
From Luke 1:46-55

46. Our community speaks; We proclaim the love of God and

47. Our hearts are filled with joy; Because God has been with us in our struggles and

48. the powerful will call us a joyful people for they will recognize our freedom and blessings;

49. He brings justice and peace (Shalom) to the oppressed;

50. Our ancestors have known Him as Holy, as we know Him and our people honor Him;

51. He stretches His powerful arms and liberates us from the clutches and snares of the power brokers – those who rob the afflicted and needy;

52. He brings down bankers, developers, oil barons, and raises our barrios and ghettos;

53. He fills our hungry with good things and the rich, He sends away empty;

54. He keeps His promise to Juan Diego, Eleonor [sic] Roosevelt, Martin Luther King and

55. will be with us forever: [111]

Elsewhere in the booklet, readers are instructed to rewrite the parable of the Good Samaritan and the story of the Crucifixion "to make it fit the world you know today."

The other Alinskyian organizing networks are just as invested in liberationism as the IAF. Liberationists Dennis Jacobsen and Cornell West are on **Gamaliel's** "First Year Reading List for New Organizers."[112] Dennis Jacobsen is the director of the Gamaliel National Clergy Caucus,[113] and a Lutheran pastor in Milwaukee. His book, *Doing Justice*, was published in 2001, based on presentations Jacobsen has made at Gamaliel's clergy-training center.[114]

The **PICO** website is rife with liberationist articles and speeches. One, delivered at a PICO conference, twists Jesus' commissioning of 70 men to spread the gospel of salvation through the forgiveness of sin into a confirmation of PICO's materialistic vision, including the discovery that Jesus "offers a three-part social program" consisting of relationship (table fellowship), addressing self-interest (curing the sick and addressing poverty), and making hope real (announcing that the kingdom of God is near).[115]

---

[111] Timothy Matovina CSB, "Blessed Are the Christian Peacemakers, For They Shall Confront the Unjust," MACC publication, 1983. "Dedicated to the Industrial Areas Foundation, Citizens Organized for Public Service of San Antonio…", Foreword, Preface, and pp 9, 14-15, 18. The "booklet arose out of a course on peace and justice in the New Testament. This course took place at the Mexican American Cultural Center in San Antonio, Texas from June 14-18, 1982. The course was led by Father John Linskens, CICM…[and] by Mr. Ernesto Cortes, a National Staff member of the Industrial Areas Foundation…" (Preface)
[112] www.gamaliel.org/Employment/neworgreadlist.htm; Jacobsen's book *Doing Justice: Congregations and Community Organizing*, says that Gamaliel is the only network to have an organized and staffed national Clergy Caucus. (p. 26)
[113] www.gamaliel.org/CRI/DIRECTORY/GNCCbd.htm
[114] Bill Wylie-Kellermann, Book Review of *Doing Justice: Congregations and Community Organizing* by Dennis Jacobsen. (Augsburg Fortress: 2001), for *Sojourners Magazine*, Nov/Dec 2001.
[115] "A Reflection on Congregation…," p 6-7.

DART is just as problematic. One of its supporters explains that the network "has a very strong biblical training component that includes how to read and use the Bible to do social analysis and to work for corporate and social reform in cities through community organizing. Its annual Clergy Conference is a continuing means for honing biblical interpretation and organizing skills of its pastors and church leaders."[116] The DART website provides ample liberationist materials to assist in this training, including a set of "Biblical reflections on God's call to do justice," tailored to clergy from various faith perspectives. [117]

This isn't Christian theology – it's a Marxist perversion.

---

[116] Robert C. Linthicum, *Building a People of Power: Equipping Churches to Transform Their Communities*, Biblica, 2006.
[117] www.thedartcenter.org/justice.html All quotes in this section come from here.

A local IAF-trained clergyman, Rev. Johnny Youngblood, from New York, was the bluntest of all: "We are not a grassroots organization. Grass roots are shallow roots. Grass roots are fragile roots. Our roots are deep roots."[118]

Being "grassroots" can mean several different things. It could mean that the group is founded at the inspiration of local people. Since Alinskyian organizations target areas in which they want to organize, obviously, their affiliates aren't grassroots in that sense.

Nor are they grassroots in the sense that local organizing is primarily about local issues or about giving local people a voice in their own governance.

The Southwest Organizing Project (SWOP) is an institutional member of the Chicago IAF, United Power for Action and Justice (UPAJ). On May 17, 2011, SWOP co-hosted an immigration rally in support of the Illinois DREAM Act (acronym for Development, Relief and Education for Alien Minors), Smart Enforcement Act, and retention of the Immigrant Services Line.[119]

- The DREAM Act creates scholarships for undocumented students;[120]
- The Smart Enforcement Act challenges existing federal immigration law that prioritizes the removal of criminal aliens posing a threat to public safety and to repeat immigration violators;[121] and
- The Immigrant Services Line Item is the part of the State of Illinois budget that specifically provides funding for immigrant needs such as emergency food, healthcare, domestic violence assistance, U.S. citizenship assistance, economic development programs, English classes, and so forth, without reference to immigration status.

Whether or not one agrees with any or all of the above provisions as they apply to illegal immigrants, each provision is a very specific *political* position...as opposed to a *moral* principle.

The moral principle here is that the United States as a nation and as individual citizens must be law-abiding and generous toward all those we encounter. Legal status doesn't change that principle.

"Generosity," however, isn't a morally defined quantity. All sorts of factors measure it, which is why "free" nations have political "conversations" about public "generosity." What level of "generosity" can the country afford? Is the country taking care of those for whom it's

---

[118] Harry Boyte, *Commonwealth: A Return to Citizen Politics*, Free Press, NY, 1990, quoting IAF leader Rev. Johnny Ray Youngblood at an IAF local (*East Brooklyn Congregations*) rally in Brooklyn.
[119] SWOP news article, "The Southwest Organizing Project (SWOP) hosts a powerful immigration rally at St. Nicholas of Tolentine Church," 5-17-11: www.swopchicago.org/display.aspx?pointer=10495
[120] The Illinois DREAM Act was signed into law in August 2011.
[121] U.S. Immigration and Customs Enforcement (ICE) information about "Secure Communities," the specific initiative targeted by the proposed "Smart Enforcement Act:"www.ice.gov/secure_communities

already responsible? Is this "generosity" inviting abuse? Are other moral principles, such as the duty to protect one's country or one's family, being sacrificed to fulfill the principle of "generosity?" How do we satisfy the tension between these principles?

In such a case, there are different good answers – that is, people of good will, coming from varying perspectives may feel a DREAM Act is politically sound while the proposed Smart Enforcement Act is suicidal.

Church social teaching wisely makes the distinction between principles and the wide gamut of political positions that are crafted, in varying times and places, to address those principles. When religious institutions get too politically embroiled, people often confuse principle with application. Knowing what good they intend, it's difficult for them to comprehend that a program to support that good could be anything but good itself.

But it happens.

Frequently.

So, the Church places political action into the hands of citizens rather than churchmen. We read, for instance:

The lay faithful are called to identify steps that can be taken in concrete political situations in order to put into practice the principles and values proper to life in society. This calls for a method of discernment, at both the personal and community levels, structured around certain key elements: knowledge of the situations, analyzed with the help of the social sciences and other appropriate tools; systematic reflection on these realities in the light of the unchanging message of the Gospel and the Church's social teaching; identification of choices aimed at assuring that the situation will evolve positively…. However, an absolute value must never be attributed to these choices because no problem can be solved once and for all.[122]

The problem with Alinskyian organizations is that they have seized the resource of the religious institution – the church or the mosque or the schul – and used its moral authority to press their own political applications. The DREAM Act becomes A Moral Mandate. Comprehensive sex-ed with its contraceptive-pushing elements becomes A Moral Mandate.

Meanwhile, the individual Catholic or Jew or Presbyterian who disagrees suddenly discovers that – without having voted for this representation (and sometimes without even *knowing* about it) – he is represented by SWOP or UPAJ or some other faith-based community organization as supporting many political positions, whether or not they offend his own political sensibilities and, most egregiously, sometimes when it vitiates genuine moral principles.

Without a vote.

Without a choice.

Often, without *knowing*.

---

[122] *Compendium of the Social Doctrine of the Church*, §568

Alinskyian organizations are also not grassroots in the sense that their organizing efforts are only superficially concerned with local needs. Ernesto Cortes, the IAF's southwestern regional director, wrote:

> The organizer's......issue gets dealt with last. If you want your issue to be dealt with first, you'll never build anything. So you lead with other people's issues, and you teach them how to act on their issues. Then you model what is to be reciprocal, you model what it is to have a long-term vision.[123]

That "long-term vision" – the organizer's "issues" that get dealt with last – is the reason for the organization. If the neighborhood gets some money to fix streets, people will be grateful to the organization and all the more willing to trust it and work with it...but fixing streets isn't the organizer's issue. That's the "other people's issue."

The *organizer's* issue is political power to create social change.

So, Alinskyian organizing isn't about giving the "little guy" civic tools to fight city hall on behalf of his own "self-interest." The little guy's "self-interest" has already been determined by the organizer and that the civic tools in which the little guy is trained are no more than rubber stamps for national programs.

In Arizona, there are several IAF locals in the major cities and one state-wide entity. Along with Arizona's Republican Governor Jan Brewer, most of the state's Democrats, and a few Republican legislators, the IAF was pushing for Medicaid expansion in 2012. This was a sensitive issue on two fronts. Some states were demonstrating their displeasure with the massive health care restructuring mandated by the Affordable Health Care Act by resisting implementation of one of the bill's "milestones," which is Medicaid expansion. A recent Supreme Court decision gave states the right to opt out of expanding coverage without penalty.

The more disturbing factor in all this, however, is that the expansion included "the mandated funding of Planned Parenthood and its involvement in therapeutic abortion."[124]

Brewer, however, attended a panel of "city, state, faith, and education leaders" hosted by one of the IAF affiliates to support the state's Medicaid expansion and also took part in a series of rallies at the State Capitol.[125] One state senator quipped that, while he didn't expect anyone's mind to be changed, "If you don't have these kinds of gatherings, organizations lose momentum."

Comments like this, of course, make opponents of the Affordable Care Act crazy: "So why is the ragtag band of Brewer [and others]... enlisting the aid of a Marxist based community

---

[123] Ernesto Cortes, "Organizing the Community: The Industrial Areas Foundation Organizer Speaks to Farmers and Farm Activists," The Texas Observer - A Journal of Free Voice, July 11, 1986.

[124] Constance Uribe, "A governor caves on Obamacare: Medicaid expansion could cost Arizonans plenty," The Washington Times, 5-28-13.

[125] Diana Martinez, "McComish voices support for governor's Medicaid expansion," *Ahwatukee Foothills News*, 5-6-13.

organizers?" [126] The question is why would *conservatives* work with progressives to help implement what they believe is a disastrous new direction for the American government? "While Governors of states like Florida, with legislators rejecting Obamacare, are facing the fact there is a system of checks and balances and branches of government are indeed separate – Arizona's Governor Brewer refuses to accept the fact that the public, including Democrats, overwhelmingly reject Obamacare and any new taxes."[127]

The point (besides observing that the progressive Alinskyian organizing networks are solidly consistent in their promotion of big government, progressive programs) is that in order to promote these programs, they must create "momentum" at the local level. This is something very different from grassroots activism.

In grassroots activism, ordinary people discover common concerns among fellow citizens and act upon those concerns. Alinskyian organizations, by contrast, have wide-scoped goals that they maneuver local people to support. The country becomes a chessboard on which local pieces are moved to bring about the greatest effect. What could be more effective than to demoralize its conservative elements by bringing the state into greater compliance with Obamacare by means of what conservatives imagine is "their" party?

If the rallies and panel discussions to expand Medicaid were *really* examples of grassroots activism, they would be confined to Arizona. The fact that they are popping up wherever one finds conservative resistance to the Affordable Care Act demonstrates their orchestrated nature. So, in Texas, IAF locals coordinated with the Network of Texas Organizations (the statewide IAF), bussing protestors to the state capitol.[128] In Ohio, Ari Lipman, lead organizer Cleveland's IAF affiliate, is also chair of the Northeast Ohio Medicaid Expansion Coalition.[129] Affiliate volunteers announced that they would be going "door to door in the legislative swing districts of Rocky River, Berea and Solon this week to urge people to contact their legislators".[130]

Of course, not every state has a strong IAF presence. The main Alinskyian organizing networks tend to have distinct territories and there were *seven* Republican governors targeted in this endeavor.[131] Gordon Whitman, the PICO National Network's Director of Policy, wrote in 2012 that over the next two years, PICO would be doing "a lot of organizing ... in the refusal states to engage and connect low-income families that have the most at stake with hospital, small

---

[126] Ibid..

[127] "Occupy Arizona? Brewer & McComish Rally Progressives against the Legislators?" *Foundation for Responsible Accountable Government* blog, 5-8-13.

[128] Dave Montgomery, "Network of Texas Organizations Rally Again for Medicaid Expansion" *Star Telegram*, 3-6-13.

[129] Abby Goodnough, "Governors Fall Away in G.O.P. Opposition to More Medicaid," *New York Times*, 2-21-13.

[130] Sarah Jane Tribble, "Could Medicaid expansion decrease drug court costs, save local taxpayer dollars? Cleveland judge says yes," *The Plain Dealer*, 5-21-13.

[131] "Governors Fall Away in G.O.P...."

business and faith groups to build the political will for Medicaid expansion."[132] An example of that has been PICO's United Florida which signed petitions to the state's governor.[133]

In Wisconsin, Citizen Action and Gamaliel are working with other progressive organizations to force their governor "to accept the federal Medicaid expansion dollars."[134] Missouri's Gamaliel organized an April 16, 2013 "bus trip to Jefferson City to meet with legislators and rally on the Capitol steps" to show support for Medicaid expansion.[135] Michigan's Gamaliel roused the troops by holding a fundraiser to send representatives to Washington, DC who would "advocate for the preservation of Medicaid" – as if failure to approve Medicaid expansion threatened the program's very existence.

Alinskyian organizations were major supporters of a nationalized health care system. Their lack of concern about its moral ramifications for the preborn child or for people severely compromised by health problems or for the elderly has been shaped by a progressive perspective that denies the "personhood" of the preborn child who can therefore be "terminated" or used for some other advantage. It measures human worth in terms of productivity and therefore has no qualms about advancing a scale of care determined by a patient's statistical likelihood of recovery…a scale that increasingly includes "right to die" options at its extreme end.

Given that commitment, one can understand that, *of course*, Alinskyian organizations would take the next step of resisting any efforts to curtail their legislative coup. However, given that many Alinskyian community organizations operate within *Catholic* parishes – which doctrinally support very different values – their work takes on a particularly sinister nature. The bishops may decry the inhumanity and disfiguring elements of the Affordable Care Act and its supportive mandates but, when they are simultaneously supporting those who have worked long and hard to assure these elements

> *Alinskyian organizations were major supporters of a nationalized health care system. Their lack of concern about its moral ramifications for the preborn child or for people severely compromised by health problems or for the elderly has been shaped by a progressive perspective that denies the "personhood" of the preborn child who can therefore be "terminated" or used for some other advantage. It measures human worth in terms of productivity and therefore has no qualms about advancing a scale of care determined by a patient's statistical likelihood of recovery…a scale that increasingly includes "right to die" options at its extreme end. …. The bishops may decry the inhumanity and disfiguring elements of the Affordable Care Act and its supportive mandates but, when they are simultaneously supporting those who have worked long and hard to assure these elements remain operative, those cries seem disingenuous…or desperately ignorant.*

---

[132] Gordon Whitman, "Governors Who Refuse Medicaid Expansion Put Politics Ahead of People," *Huffington Post* Politics Blog, 7-24-12.

[133] PICO's Florida United Facebook page: See May 10 link to: petitions.moveon.org/sign/tell-governor-scott-in/?source=search. See also Facebook entries April 23, April 25, May 1; John Kennedy, "Loaves, fishes and Medicaid expansion cited by clergy," *Palm Beach Post*, Post on Politics blog, 3-20-13.

[134] Brian Sikma, "Citizen Action Medicaid Expansion Endorsement Reads like Political Roster," mediatrackers, 5-13-13.

[135] Spencer Barrett, "MCU Medicaid Expansion: Fill Up the Buses," Gamaliel website, 4-16-13.

remain operative, those cries seem disingenuous…or desperately ignorant.

The website of the Episcopal Church of the Good Samaritan in Clearwater, Florida carries information about Faith and Action for Strength Together *(FAST),* which is a congregation-based community organization in Pinellas County, Florida, operating within the DART network. The page concerning FAST states: "The organization is not political but rather, it is biblical."[136]

This assertion is echoed in other places. Rev. Willie McClendon Jr., a minister at Shiloh Missionary Baptist Church who co-founded FAST, also insists that the organization is "Biblical and not political" but simultaneously says, "There is power in numbers. Politicians look at it in terms of (potential) votes."[137] Despite protestations to the contrary, it really *is* about politics.

A local news article reported that FAST "managed to wrest commitments from city and county officials to build 3,000 new low-cost housing units within three years. Since its founding in 2004, the group counts new bus shelters and funding for prekindergarten programs among its victories."[138] What does FAST think politics is if this isn't political?

> *Despite protestations to the contrary, [Alinskyian organizing] really is about politics…. Of* course *this is political activity.*

Since when isn't politics about establishing public policy? Since when isn't it about getting laws passed? Since when isn't it about allocating public money for particular projects…and therefore not allocating money for other things? Since when isn't politics about getting people elected who support you in the endeavors that one believes will best serve the common good?

Of *course* this is political activity.

When DART, with FAST in attendance, holds a public accountability session to shame or pressure St. Petersburg's deputy mayor to support its Construction Incentive Project (CIP),[139] it is engaging in political activity. When FAST pushes for a new "local hiring law,"[140] it's engaged in political activity. When FAST boasts that, because it lobbied all seven county commissioners to support an affordable housing trust fund, "$19.2 million has been allocated to the fund,"[141] it is engaging in political activity.

---

[136] Good Samaritan Episcopal website: www.goodsamaritan-swfla.org/fast.htm
[137] Amy Mormino, "Faith in Action: FAST of Pinellas County," The *St. Petersburg Christianity Examiner,* 5-24-11.
[138] Sherri Day, "Religion Spiced with Politics," *Tampa Bay Times,* 3-17-07.
[139] Mitch Perry, "FAST movers*," Creative Loafing Tampa – Political Animal,* 4-17-14.
[140] Mark Puente, "St. Petersburg considers $150,000 study on local hiring practices," *Tampa Bay Times,* 11-18-12.
[141] DART website, page about FAST: thedartcenter.org/location/fast/#sthash.oYSdY3VI.dpuf

FAST's 2012 501c-3 form states that FAST engages in political lobbying. It states that FAST attempted to influence legislation through direct contact with public officials and through rallies and similar activity.[142] That's *political* activity.

So, why does FAST claim that it isn't political when its political activity is in the public eye, a fact for anyone to see?

The answer is that it's playing politics and the political activity of religious institutions is dangerous business.

Whether or not FAST is on the best side of a given political issue, the fact that its advocacy never concerns doctrinally-defined moral principles. Rather, it is only about *applications* of those principles. This means that there will always be fellow congregants among FAST member churches who are at odds with FAST's agenda. To force dissenting congregants into political support of a "prudential" position – an application – of principles about which they have every legal and moral right to disagree[143] is an abuse of religion. Congregational membership in FAST is, therefore, abusive and divisive.

The fact that FAST is engaged in political activity and exists for no other reason than to engage in political activity, brings religious institutions into an uncomfortable relationship with the IRS, too. Therefore a sort of "mental reservation" is required that redefines "engaging in political activity" or "being a political organization" to mean "engaging in *partisan* political activity" or "being a *partisan* political organization." The word partisan must be redefined, too because if one observes that all of FAST's political activity serves progressive (statist) applications, FAST argues "partisan" means "Republican Party" or "Democrat Party."[144]

FAST's secretary, Rabbi Torop, expresses it this way: "We are quite clearly and emphatically non partisan and non political. We neither endorse nor advise any particular candidates. When it comes to a particular election, we look to find allies and partners in government entities who want to solve the same problems we want to solve, and with whom we can find agreement on the kind of solutions that are the most appropriate and achievable. We are very careful to be non political **in that sense**."[145] [emphasis added]

The sense in which FAST is non-political is *very* narrow. To further its self-interest, FAST requires its own lexicon.

---

[142] FAST 2012 tax form: pdfs.citizenaudit.org/2010_10_EO/20-2058779_990EZ_200912.pdf

[143] FAST, like all faith-based Alinskyian organizations, has only institutional members. If Good Samaritan Episcopal is a member of FAST, then its entire congregation is considered to support FAST's agenda when FAST confronts public officials or issues public statements. Furthermore, FAST is supported by a percentage of member-congregations' income – meaning that every tithing congregant in a FAST congregation contributes to FAST.

[144] For example, Bishop Robert Lynch's March 15, 2011 column, "Holding FAST," argues that FAST is "is neither Republican nor Democratic."

   That said, insofar as the Democrat Party at this point in time tends to be progressive, there is a natural affinity between it and FAST. So, for instance, the Largo/Mid-Pinellas Democratic Club announced a February 20, 2012 meeting to learn more about FAST from one of its organizers, "speaking to us about the outstanding work that this organization does." www.largodemocrats.com/2012/02/

[145] Jeff Solochek, "Weekend interview with Rabbi Michael Torop of Faith and Action for Strength Together," a *Tampa Bay Times*, 10-30-10.

Why on earth would a religious institution yoke itself to such a divisive, deceitful political organization?

Perhaps it is because the individuals forging that yoke share similar, partisan political perspectives.

Consider the following two expressions of civic engagement.

A: A pro-life group canvasses political candidates for the upcoming elections and, on the basis of their replies and prior voting record (if any), compiles a voters' guide detailing the pro-life positions of each candidate. A strong pro-life record or responses implies, in all likelihood, that the pro-life group and its constituency would support that candidate.

B: An interfaith coalition that desires the passage of certain education programs holds a candidates' forum, asking candidates to publicly state whether or not they will commit to those programs. A strong commitment to the coalition's programs implies, in all likelihood, that the coalition and its constituency would support that candidate.

Which is a political act?

Both are, of course.

The principle distinction between the two is that the former concerns a life and death issue, in and of itself, whereas the latter concerns support of one possible moral response to an important issue out of many possible and moral responses. That's an important distinction. However, despite their significant differences, both are – as said – political acts. The religious institution, with concerns about retaining its tax exempt status (for shame), must consider which of these two political acts it can permit on its property without endangering its immortal soul…um, its *status quo*.

Let's look at a concrete example. On October 8, 2010, Archbishop Michael Sheehan of the Roman Catholic Archdiocese of Santa Fe wrote his priests:

> Please ensure that you do not give permission to any group to distribute political materials before, during or after Mass or to place materials on cars in our parking lots. I know that many groups, (i.e., Right to Life and New Mexicans for a Moral and Constitutional Government) distribute their materials without our permission. Please monitor their activity as best you can so that we do not lose our tax exempt status.

However, a few weeks later, October 24, Albuquerque Interfaith, an IAF affiliate, held its 2010 Candidates Accountability at St. Therese Catholic Parish in the same archdiocese. Candidates were asked to ratify an agenda that included support for public schools, for the

Why on earth would a religious institution yoke itself to such a divisive, deceitful political organization?
Perhaps it is because the individuals forging that yoke share similar, partisan political perspectives.

DREAM Act, and for Lottery/Bridge Scholarships for all students "regardless of immigration status." Candidates were not permitted to discuss alternative opinions. They were only allowed a moment to express agreement (to which the audience responded with rehearsed enthusiasm) or disagreement (which brought about stony silence). This was not an unbiased, non-partisan public forum.

So, let's understand this: Right to Life materials clarifying which candidates hold positions compatible with Catholic moral teaching are impermissible politicking but holding a candidates' forum with the express intention of garnering public funding for various politically partisan programs is not only permissible but *encouraged*…on church property and orchestrated by an ecumenical group that was named in the Archdiocese's 5-year pastoral plan for "Gospel Justice."

Never mind that the standing ovations received at Albuquerque Interfaith's 2010 candidates forum – in a Catholic church – were for people with strong pro-abortion voting records. Never mind that Catholics who weren't supporters of the Albuquerque Interfaith agenda weren't welcome at the forum. This was a scripted, public event.

Oh, the Archdiocese's "Policy and Guidelines Pertaining to Prohibited Campaign Activities in the Archdiocese of Santa Fe" is very clear. Forums, even those with an express political agenda that's contrary to Catholic teaching, may be held on church property so long as all the candidates are invited. On the other hand, materials or statements made in homilies that might indirectly support a candidate or that so much as identify a candidate as "pro-life" are "not permitted."

If one had a cynical turn of mind, one might wonder if the pro-lifers held candidate forums and the political progressives distributed voter guides, rather than the other way round, how quickly there would be a sudden reversal of archdiocesan policies.

During the 2012 elections, the progressive interfaith media organization Faith in Public Life held a press conference and released a statement about a new campaign that, in the estimation of the *Los Angeles Times,* would seek "to influence the 2012 election."[146]

> *PICO National Network and Faith in Public Life wanted presidential candidates to know that its members opposed "a Republican-backed ballot measure in Minnesota that would require voters to show photo identification" and supported "the Obama health care plan, immigration reform and economic policies that would increase taxes on the wealthiest."*

---

[146] Mitchell Landsberg, "Faith-based organization seeking to promote economic equality," *Los Angeles Times*, 4-25-12.

PICO National Network and Faith in Public Life wanted presidential candidates to know that its members opposed "a Republican-backed ballot measure in Minnesota that would require voters to show photo identification" and supported "the Obama health care plan, immigration reform and economic policies that would increase taxes on the wealthiest." The *Los Angeles Times* made it clear, in case readers might miss the point: "Those are all positions, of course, that generally line up with those espoused by President Barack Obama and not by Mitt Romney."

The *Los Angeles Times* knows partisan politics when it sees it.

The organizers know it, too. To quote IAF organizer Arnold Graf, "In places like San Antonio and Baltimore, we are as close to being a political party as anybody is. We go around organizing people, getting them to agree on an agenda, registering them to vote, interviewing candidates on whether they support our agenda. We're not a political party, but that's what political parties do."[147]

To quote IAF organizer Arnold Graf, "In places like San Antonio and Baltimore, we are as close to being a political party as anybody is. We go around organizing people, getting them to agree on an agenda, registering them to vote, interviewing candidates on whether they support our agenda. We're not a political party, but that's what political parties do."

---

[147] William Greider, Who Will Tell the People, p. 224.

Mark Warren, premier author of *A Match on Dry Grass: Community Organizing as a Catalyst for School Reform* and a long-time academic apologist for Alinskyian community organizing[148], is one of the leaders of Harvard Graduate School of Education's Community Organizing and School Reform Project. The Project produced *A Match on Dry Grass* and hosted a national conference in 2012 from which it has made available materials, videos, and related publications.[149]

The title is a metaphor for a desiccated education system in which parents are frustrated and angry. In such an environment, all it takes is a small push for reform, supplied by professional organizers around the country, to ignite a wild prairie-fire of a movement against the "'savage inequalities of American public education." (p. 5)[150] At least, that's the plan.

The Project studied six locally-situated groups, four of which belong to larger, interconnected Alinskyian networks (the other two, the authors explain, have their roots in the civil rights movement but they, too, have strong Alinskyian connections). Each of these local groups operates within its own community as well as working collectively on a broader platform, through collaborations and partnerships, to promote progressive interests, among them "education reform."

> *"Community organizing groups do not engage in school reform solely for the purpose of improving public education. They work to improve public education as part of a larger process of developing leaders and building power for communities to address the full range of structural imbalances that combine to create poverty and marginalization."*

However, *A Match on Dry Grass* is clear that what the Alinskyian community organizations understand by "education reform" involves changing *many* things. "Community organizing groups do not engage in school reform solely for the purpose of improving public education. They work to improve public education as part of a larger process of developing leaders and building power for communities to address the full range of structural imbalances that combine to create poverty and marginalization."(p. 32)

In other words, progressive education reform is part of a package that has a much larger vision than merely restructuring dysfunctional school systems. Alinskyian community organizing is building a body of people who support something undefined but assuredly different. Not only is it left undefined what the end product of "systemic change" will look like but many terms are used ambiguously. When the reader is reminded of "the importance of

---

[148] Mark Warren's earlier writings include: *Fire in the Heart: How White Activists Embrace Racial Justice* (2010); *Dry Bones Rattling: Community Building to Revitalize American Democracy* (2001); and *Social Capital and Poor Communities* (2005).

[149] The website is: matchondrygrass.org.

[150] All page numbers are from *A Match on Dry Grass,* unless otherwise noted.

involving families in the education of their children," it's likely that he will imagine parents who read to their children, who supervise homework, and who examine report cards with genuine interest. He may think of parents who are active in Parent-Teacher Associations or who volunteer in their children's classrooms.

This is not what Alinskyian community organizations mean when they "involve families" in their children's education. *Alinskyian-trained* parents are engaged as "change agents who can transform urban schools and neighborhoods" (quoting educator Dennis Shirley). The Alinskyian community organizations are only superficially about education; they are "*primarily* political, albeit normally nonpartisan, organizations focused on institutional change."(p. 7, emphasis added) This means that Alinskyian organizations supplant conventional political and social processes with their own agenda: "Organizing groups become an active agent in this historic and ongoing process, providing a vehicle for people to build the capacity of their community."[151] (p. 21) This is accomplished by teaching trainees, ironically called "leaders,"[152] to do the political work that has been predetermined by the organization: "All [Alinskyian organizing] groups train emerging leaders in the operation of political systems so people can develop strategies to effect change. Using political education or other means, organizing groups also help leaders place their current struggles in the context of larger historic efforts with their community, whether as people of faith committed to social justice [or] as African-Americans struggling for freedom." (p. 29)

> *"All [Alinskyian organizing] groups train emerging leaders in the operation of political systems so people can develop strategies to effect change."*

"Leaders" are also reeducated to understand their problems from a specifically progressive-political worldview: Organizing groups "work with communities to reshape that story [their historical narrative] into a contemporary narrative concerning who they are today, what they are organizing for and why their cause is just." (pp. 30-31)

With this introduction, the study turns to its six examples of advocacy for education "reform," four of which are by Alinskyian groups. One, PACT in San Jose, California is affiliated with the national PICO network. Two are part of the international Industrial Areas Foundation network: One LA in Los Angeles and the Logan Square Neighborhood Association in Chicago.[153] Northwest Bronx Community and Clergy Coalition in New York City is part of the National People's Action network.[154]

---

[151] It is difficult to read this and not think of Marxism's insistence that the radical is an agent of history – *making* history rather than *reacting* to it or being subject to it.

[152] "Any participant in the organizing effort is called a leader, in recognition of their potential." (p. 30)

[153] The Logan Square Neighborhood Association is a member of the Lakeview Action Coalition which is, in turn, a member of the city-wide United Power for Action and Justice…which is an affiliate of the Industrial Areas Foundation network.

[154] The remaining two, Padres y Jóvenes Unidos in Denver and Southern Echo in the Mississippi Delta, have connections to Alinskyian organizing but are not part of the major Alinskyian organizing networks.

San Jose, California Parent-leaders of PACT fought, as they were trained, to advocate for "small-schools" having "site-based autonomy." In actuality, the "small schools" were mastery learning laboratories based on the work of Deborah Meier, whose *The Power of Their Ideas* was PACT-parent reading material.(p. 41) Mastery learning – later called *outcome based education* – is not traditional education, where a student is expected to learn specific information and skills but is *transformational*, that is, it operates from an array of predetermined outcomes, some of which are attitudinal or affective, that the student must demonstrate he has mastered. When the outcome is "to know the multiplication table," an outcome-based approach seems reasonable; when the outcome is "to accept diversity" or "to make healthful food choices" the school has overstepped its role…particularly as such outcomes can only be measured in terms of behavior.[155]

> *When the outcome is "to know the multiplication table," an outcome-based approach seems reasonable; when the outcome is "to accept diversity" or "to make healthful food choices" the school has overstepped its role…particularly as such outcomes can only be measured in terms of behavior.*

To further assure parents that the charter schools they were helping to build would be properly oriented, PACT hired a regional Coalition of Essential Schools affiliate to coach the design teams planning its charter schools. The Coalition of Essential Schools has been a prime mover of mastery learning (outcome based education).

One component of these small, mastery learning schools is community organizing. Not only was PACT a primary factor in *creating* these charter schools but it assures a continued presence by "providing" an organizer at each school site to oversee "parent engagement." (p. 59)

There is daily indoctrination of the students in PACT schools: "The principal blows a whistle, and the children organize themselves into lines of about twenty. 'Good morning, L.U.C.H.A. leaders!'" L.U.C.H.A. is the name of one of the PACT charter schools, an acronym standing for "Learning in an Urban Community with High Achievement" that means "fight" in Spanish. "Teachers and students, loudly and enthusiastically declare together, 'I am a leader in my home, in my school, and' – pointing at the neighborhood all around them in a large circle – 'in my community.' Together they recite a promise to each other to be responsible, respectful, and compassionate and –pounding their small fists into their hands enthusiastically – 'to work hard every day!'" (p. 47)

As an aside, but related to the understanding that the change sought by Alinskyian organizing efforts is far broader than merely "education," in tangent with its work to create small, mastery learning charter schools in San Jose, PACT also has expended a good deal of time and energy promoting Healthy Kids, a program to provide comprehensive medical, dental and vision

---

[155] Mastery learning (or outcome based education) is the foundation of today's Common Core movement. According to the authors of this book, "powerful forces like the Gates Foundation were pushing for small schools and small learning communities across the country." (p. 42) The Gates Foundation has been a key funder of the Common Core initiative.

insurance to children whose families don't qualify for other public programs. *Comprehensive* means, among many other things, that eligible women who are pregnant can receive all sorts of "family planning" services.[156]

Lest one be tempted to dismiss PACTs activities as limited to a few small schools, the authors of *A Match on Dry Grass* assure us that "PACT is not satisfied with creating strong cultures of academic success at individual schools; they aim to create high-quality educational options for *all* San Jose's children." (p. 64)

Los Angeles, California; Chicago, Illinois Two of the organizations *A Match on Dry Grass* studies are affiliates of the Industrial Areas Foundation – the Alinskyian organizing network founded by Saul Alinsky himself and on which PICO and the National People's Action (among others) are modeled.

The IAF's efforts for educational "reform" began in Texas with, among other things, the creation of Alliance public schools. Like PICO's model small schools in San Jose, Alliance schools are designed to be part of a larger organizational structure – themselves institutional members of their local IAF groups.(p. 70) Like PICO, IAF teaches its "leaders" to think "more broadly" about educational issues – including the environment and personal health, for example. (p. 81) Like PICO, IAF organizers work internally within each Alliance school, training teachers, principals, and parents in organizational ("relational") culture.(p. 70) Most significantly, Alliance schools are also patterned on mastery learning pedagogy.

> *PACT also has expended a good deal of time and energy promoting Healthy Kids, a program to provide comprehensive medical, dental and vision insurance to children whose families don't qualify for other public programs. Comprehensive means, among many other things, that eligible women who are pregnant can receive all sorts of "family planning" services.*

> *"PACT is not satisfied with creating strong cultures of academic success at individual schools; they aim to create high-quality educational options for all San Jose's children."*

Spreading to California, One LA organizers in Los Angeles had parents study the "Alliance strategy that worked so well in Texas," (p. 72) namely by growing "a new political constituency" (p. 73) Interested principals attended IAF training and brought organizers into their schools to work among parents and teachers. (p. 84) They were taught how to handpick "leadership" (p. 86) among teachers and parents and then test these "leaders" in small actions that serve several purposes. One is, of course, to make some small, immediate improvement in the school environment. The more important purpose, however, is to build the organization's base of support:

---

[156] The Santa Clara Healthy Kids (which includes San Jose) website enumerates its services: www.scfhp.com/programs-and-services/healthy-kids (accessed August 23, 2013; no longer available).

"Through community meetings and planning sessions, Harmony parents like Benitez step forward and demonstrate the kind of desire and temperament One LA looks for in leaders. Harmony staff and organizer Fujimoto identify these parents and focus their energy on developing them as leaders."(p. 92)

The *ultimate* goal is "influencing educational change and civic life" (p. 96) and while *A Match on Dry Grass* contrasts the IAF's relation-building "to more mainstream education reform that seeks to implement single-focus reform strategies," (p. 97) the end is the same: a comprehensive system of education, womb-to-tomb health care, and workforce development.

The Chicago public school district was among the first to experiment with mastery learning – and the result was disastrous.[157] Blaming disunity among implementing parties rather than the pedagogy itself, groups such as the Logan Square Neighborhood Association (LSNA) in Chicago – who are committed to the progressive restructuring of education – worked at building trust with parents, students, teachers, and administrators. (p. 172) This gave them a base from which to launch a "Holistic Plan" that resolved, among other things, to "develop schools as community centers" and "support community controlled education." (p. 173) To these ends, LSNA worked to transform area schools into "community learning centers," which in addition to educating children, provides childcare for adults who study English and earn their GEDs, as well as offering an array of after-school enrichment programs for their students.

LSNA also has a parent mentor program, training some to become full-time, paid organizers. Special week-long sessions for parents who showing particular aptitude are arranged to teach them the "praxis of community organizing as well as an understanding of power and accountability within the community context. Participants analyze community power dynamics, examine forms of accountability, explore the nature of publicly accountable and private relationships, and analyze their own strengths and weaknesses in the public sphere. For a culminating training project, leaders design an action plan that would push an elected official toward a vote change." (p. 184)

By placing the school at the center of community life, LSNA introduces parents to a wide-range of issues – "immigration reform, health, safety, and housing. It does this through weekly training sessions at each school, neighborhood-wide parent mentor workshops across the schools, and one-on-one conversations between organizers and parents." (p. 191) While *A Match on Dry Grass* doesn't believe that LSNA is in a position to "directly address teaching and learning," it believes "success stories" are needed to "drive school reform and practice," which they do by breaking down traditional educational approaches and by developing a supportive population.

The interesting thing in all this is that while the rhetoric from LSNA about school reform supports "community controlled" schools, the five school-based Community Learning Centers it

---

[157] For one account, see: Anthony S. Bryk, "Social Trust: A Moral Resource for School Improvement," The University of Chicago Center for School Improvement and Barbara Schneider NORC and The University of Chicago, June, 1996. Bryk writes: "Many of the major reform initiatives advanced in urban school districts during the 1980s failed. For example, a systemwide mastery learning curriculum in Chicago was ill conceived and poorly implemented."

has developed – like every other public school in the Chicago system – are plugged into Common Core[158] – a nationally-controlled system of education.

New York City Northwest Bronx Community and Clergy Coalition in New York City is part of the National People's Action network. The Coalition began in the 1970s as a response to tenant-landlord problems, operating from an Alinskyian community organizing tradition. (p. 202) Two decades later, its focus shifted to education – more than understandable in an area with massive high school dropout rates and tremendous school overcrowding. Besides the obvious physical improvements their schools needed, which became the media "frame" for their actions (p. 208) the Coalition worked with the Annenberg Institute for School Reform (p. 209), one of the key backers of mastery learning in the country. To draw more government money into the schools, the Coalition became a founding member of the Alliance for Quality Education, a statewide education movement that supports Common Core,[159] discourages traditional standardized tests in favor of Common Core assessments,[160] and encourages embedding community organizations within schools "in order to sustain school change."[161] It is also important that these reformed schools include "wraparound supports for students"[162] The Coalition is obviously an important component in this: "Organizing groups have been successful at breaking down many barriers to strong school-community relationships."[163] Besides its work for universal reform, the Coalition has also focused on creating a model high school, The Leadership Institute, which is an

> *Students [at the Leadership Institute] are given hands-on training in organizing, learning how to mobilize, how to identify allies, and how to work with the media.*

"organizing and social justice themed small school."(p. 212) Students are given hands-on training in organizing, learning how to mobilize, how to identify allies, and how to work with the media. (p. 213) Annenberg researchers found that "the school stands as a testament to young people's desire for quality education in the Bronx and provides evidence that when students are given support and respect, they can and will get engaged in a deep and sustained way in the work of education reform." [164]

It's notable that there's no mention of academic achievement in this reform effort. New schools have been built, curriculum has been redesigned, and parents are deeply engaged but...*to what end*? "The Coalition uses ongoing campaigns and individual actions as vehicles by which to identify and test new leaders and also to engage in purposeful, ongoing mentorship and

---

[158] http://www.cps.edu/commoncore/pages/commoncore.aspx

[159] Alliance for Quality Education website, "quality curriculum": http://www.aqeny.org/wp-content/uploads/2013/08/Quality-Curriculum.pdf

[160] Alliance for Quality Education website, position on testing: http://www.aqeny.org/wp-content/uploads/2011/01/Testing-position.pdf

[161] Alliance for Quality Education website, parent-family engagement: http://www.aqeny.org/ny/wp-content/uploads/2011/01/PARENT-FAMILY-ENGAGEMENT1.pdf

[162] Ibid.

[163] Ibid.

[164] http://annenberginstitute.org/sites/default/files/product/236/files/Mott_Bronx_Summary.pdf

training with their current core leaders." (p 217) There are "robust" leadership trainings and much relationship-building but the "frame" through which all this energy is expended – namely, overcrowded schools and therefore a system "designed to fail" – misses the more salient problem of undereducated students.

In Summary While there are differences among the various community organizations examined in *A Match on Dry Grass,* the common transformational aspirations of the organizers are much deeper than their "leadership" understands. Each of the four Alinskyian organizations – though part of different networks and proposing programs with different names – are working toward exactly the same end: a national education system that ties schooling to work within a comprehensive package of welfare and healthcare.

The underbrush of tradition – of autonomous parents, of subsidiary local schooling, of self-governing communities – is swept away and planted, in its stead, is a cooperative, managed citizenry.

The authors of this work appreciate that "[c]ommunity organizing groups also operate in larger systems of policy discourse where resourceful networks are advocating specific reform plans. Indeed, we stressed above that organizing is not an entirely grassroots phenomenon and that organizing groups receive input from multiple levels as they respond to opportunities in the institutional or policy context. Some readers may be concerned about the alignment of certain initiatives with neoliberal reform agendas." (pp. 260-261)

But, despite the common "outcome" realized by each of the four Alinskyian groups, *A Match on Dry Grass* misses what each has actually accomplished.

Perhaps no word is as telling as "partnership." Parents, in each of the examples studied, are redefined as "partners" with teachers and students and politicians. They are brought to understand themselves as part of a "collaborative process" in which they "participate." Community organizers artfully leverage social pressure to unify all players around widely-accepted goals (e.g., more school buildings, smaller classrooms) while taking attention away from more controversial aspects of their desired "reform" (e.g., Common Core).

The organizers have put a match to the dry grass of parental frustration and are monitoring a controlled burn. The underbrush of tradition – of autonomous parents, of subsidiary local schooling, of self-governing communities – is swept away and planted, in its stead, is a cooperative, managed citizenry.

If you happen to be in a congregation that's part of an Alinskyian community organization, there will be "house meetings."

The organizer running the show will ask attendees what concerns they have for their neighborhood. The organizers are looking for specific answers: unemployment, lack of adequate healthcare insurance, school issues…something like that.

Every once in a while, the organizer will get someone in the crowd who wants to do something about abortion. He will be told, "That's too divisive an issue. We only get involved with issues we can all agree on."

Universal healthcare – all Americans agree that the federal government should guarantee healthcare to everyone living within its borders, regardless of abortion provisions buried within them. Right? Evidently, that's what the Alinskyian community organizing networks contend.

The PICO National Network was the most aggressively active in touting health care issues with abortion components. In California, PICO's earlier efforts included a successful legislative push to fund a mobile medical van providing school-based health care and Planned Parenthood referrals. Some California PICO congregations were sites for Healthy Families, as well, providing elective abortion and family planning coverage.

When the Affordable Health Care Act was under consideration, PICO and other organizations ran TV ad campaigns (one under the moniker of "People of Faith for Health Reform") organized nationwide prayer events, and recommended a "health care sermon weekend."

The message, said PICO spokesman Gordon Whitman, is this: 'Religious voters support health-care reform, and you can't take them for granted. We're not going to allow people who stand up for health reform to be attacked on religious grounds. If you are in a district or state that is culturally conservative, there is support for health reform.' In August, paid organizers will meet with pastors to help them organize their congregations, develop talking points for meetings with members of Congress and coordinate with other groups and individuals -- religious and secular.[165]

Abortion provisions were no obstacle to PICO's support for healthcare reform. "To hold together their diverse memberships," the above PICO statement continues, "the coalitions are moving carefully around controversial issues. For example…PICO [is] supporting the 'status quo' on abortion – neither requiring nor banning insurers from covering the procedure as long as federal funds are not used."

The Gamaliel Network also pushed nationalized health care. Its 2009 website carried the gleeful information:

---

[165] PICO National Network, "Pulling Together on Health Care," *Washington Post*, July 25, 2009

Barack H. Obama, former GAMALIEL ORGANIZER is the 44th President of the United States!" and announces that on June 22-25, 2009, it bussed in hundreds of clergy and leaders from across the country to Washington DC for visits to congressional representatives to discuss health care. "The Gamaliel National Clergy Caucus is leading Gamaliel's newest national issue: Health Care. They invite you and your spiritual community to discuss and then act on their latest theological statement.

Gamaliel was part of the *Health Care for America Now* coalition that included several other Alinskyian organizing networks, such as the now-defunct ACORN, as well as some pro-abortion groups like the Religious Coalition for Reproductive Choice and Planned Parenthood Federation of America. And DART – the Direct Action and Research Training Center – website claimed that its local affiliates were responsible for accessible health care reform in several major metropolitan cities.[166]

The Industrial Areas Foundation (IAF), as a national body, kept a lower profile on its support of universal health care than the other Alinskyian networks. However, it was among the "allies" of Jobs with Justice, in a national "Health Care for All" campaign, with all its abortion-friendly elements.

Several IAF *affiliates*, on the other hand, were right in the middle of the health care fracas. United Power for Action and Justice, a Chicago monster-organization with hundreds of institutional members, fought for statewide healthcare in Illinois. "Because of a relationship that was built with Illinois Governor Rod Blagoiavich, UPAJ was in a good position to work with him to achieve affordable, quality healthcare for all Illinois residents," writes Lynn Wax, an UPAJ leader.[167]

BUILD, the IAF local of Baltimore, was part of the *Health Care for All* coalition pushing for universal health care in Maryland, organized specifically to support Maryland Citizens' Health Initiative…which was, in turn, part of the abortion-inclusive *Health Care for America Now* coalition.

The *Greater Boston Interfaith Organization* (GBIO) was another IAF active in healthcare activism. "GBIO and the Affordable Care Today Coalition have played a critical role in making health care reform in Massachusetts a reality," the 2009 GBIO website stated. "We will continue to make sure that this historic reform is implemented fairly and completely."

The "historic reform" under discussion is the Massachusetts Health Reform Law that GBIO fought to implement and it has several interesting components. One is that family planning services are universally provided throughout the state.[168]

"Family planning" is catch-all phrase that, at a minimum refers to contraception – many forms of which are abortifacient – and often includes abortion "services." Mike Huckabee,

---

[166] DART website: thedartcenter.org/learn-about-dart
[167] "Making a Difference on Healthcare," Prophetic Voices, Jewish Funds for Justice newsletter, Summer 2007.
[168] Families USA Report, "Massachusetts Health Reform of 2006," pp 6-7.

former governor of Arkansas, says, "The Massachusetts model [of universal health care provision] has been a total disaster. It's been a disaster from a financial standpoint, [and is] about to bankrupt that state....It gives people the opportunity to have an abortion for a $50 co-pay, so that's all that a human life is worth now in Massachusetts - $50."[169]

Yet this is what the GBIO – including its Catholic members – has proudly promoted. "[T]he push for the new law and the debate over its implementation have provided a chance to prove that religious groups can be marshaled behind liberal issues at a time when faith is more commonly associated with conservative social causes, such as the campaign against same-sex marriage. 'It's a tremendous story about the power of the pews to organize for justice — and particularly, the Jewish pews,' said Rabbi Jonah Pesner, who helped head the interfaith coalition [GBIO] from his post as a religious leader of Temple Israel, a Reform synagogue in Boston. Pesner recently assumed leadership of the Union for Reform Judaism's new Just Congregations initiative, which aims to replicate the successes achieved in Boston."[170]

This "power of the pews to organize" rests in the hands of the organizers. "Hamilton and Pesner, of Temple Israel in Boston, are leaders of the *Greater Boston Interfaith Organization*, which has used moral suasion to become an influential force in Beacon Hill's healthcare debate. Inside the velvet glove, though, is a real threat: If legislators don't pass a healthcare bill to their liking, the group and its allies will push a 2006 ballot measure that would force the state to cover everybody. Backers of the ballot effort have collected more than 112,000 signatures."[171]

In the words of one enamored blogger, "Forget about the symbolic politics on the religious right and the religious left for a minute. Here's a story about a local coalition of religious organizations that crosses denominational, theological, and political lines and that is exerting real political pressure on the Massachusetts legislature to bring healthcare to more people." [172]

"Exerting real political pressure" makes GBIO a real political organization with a real political agenda. *The Jewish Daily Forward* article quoted above described a speech of then-Illinois Democratic Senator Barack Obama "at a conference of the liberal religious group Call to Renewal. Obama chastised fellow Democrats for failing to 'acknowledge the power of faith in the lives of the American people' and insisted that the party

> *Real progressive political pressure, leveraged with the support of religious bodies, while vitiating their core moral values...now that's Alinskyian organizing for you.*

compete for the support of religiously observant Americans. He also called for liberals to moderate their opposition to faith-based initiatives and to some expressions of religion in public life....'I cannot overplay the extent to which the Obama speech is still on people's minds,' said

---

[169] Steven Ertelt, "Mike Huckabee Calls Barack Obama Most Pro-Abortion President in History," *Life News,* 8-6-09
[170] Jennifer Siegel, "Religious Liberals Take Lead in Massachusetts Health Debate, *The Jewish Daily Forward,* July 21, 2006
[171] Scott S. Greenberger, "Interfaith leaders invoke morality in healthcare debate, Boston Globe, 12-29-05.
[172] Philocrites, "'Coalition of compassion' has clout on Beacon Hill," 1-4-06, www.philocrites.com/archives/002445.html

Mik Moore, director of communications of the anti-poverty organization Jewish Funds for Justice."

Real progressive political pressure, leveraged with the support of religious bodies, while vitiating their core moral values…now that's Alinskyian organizing for you.

In the final months before the Affordable Care Act was passed, the PICO National Network, Gamaliel, and a number of other groups formed the *We Believe Together - Health Care for All* coalition that launched a *40 Days for Health Reform* campaign. The coalition sponsored a highly publicized conference call between President Obama and the "people of faith" within its networks to discuss the issue. It also ran a nationwide TV ad, featuring clergy stumping for the bill. It prepared printed material that misapplied scripture verses, particularly Matthew 25's warning that people will "be judged by how they treat the least of these," as a scriptural mandate for their proposed health care bill. "Healing is God's desire for every person because everyone is created in the divine image."[173]

Last but not least, the coalition mobilized a "National Day of Action for Health Insurance Reform," coordinated by PICO. On August 11, 2009, various PICO locals (and a few other groups) held dozens of "prayer rallies" or "vigils" and in-district

Many of the politically-motivated "prayer vigils" were scheduled together with press conferences – no taking these prayers into the closet.

meetings to influence members of Congress about federal health care legislation. Many of the politically-motivated "prayer vigils" were scheduled together with press conferences – no taking these prayers into the closet.

For Catholics, there was a particular irony to all this. The Catholic Church is a tremendous supporter of Alinskyian community organizing. At one point, the USCCB website openly praised PICO as helping to lead the struggle for universal health care reform – a struggle that intimately effects not only Catholics who are in PICO affiliate community organizations, but also Catholics who give money to the annual Catholic collection, the *Catholic Campaign for Human Development* (CCHD), as well as Catholics who participate in its various education programs to teach social justice activism – which are highly secularized and supportive of participation in Alinskyian community organizing like PICO.

PICO and USCCB collaborated to define a position that would address access for all; and the USCCB and PICO have worked together to press Congress to protect the poor in health reform, including issuing a joint statement with other religious denominations on this issue on July 6, 2009…. The USCCB has invited PICO staff and clergy to brief

---

[173] Sojourners' Health Care Toolkit, www.sojo.net/action/alerts/health_care_toolkit.pdf

60 | P a g e

, on our health care efforts and has encouraged dioceses and parishes to work with ⌐ affiliates to hold educational sessions on health care.[174]

On the other hand, the United States Conference of Catholic Bishops insisted that it was "working to ensure that needed health reform [would not be] undermined by abandoning longstanding and widely supported policies against abortion funding and mandates and in favor of conscience protection."[175]

No one should be required to pay for or participate in abortion. It is essential that the legislation clearly apply to this new program longstanding and widely supported federal restrictions on abortion funding and mandates, and protections for rights of conscience. No current bill meets this test.... If acceptable language in these areas cannot be found, we will have to oppose the health care bill vigorously.[176]

Schizophrenic positions notwithstanding, the Affordable Care Act was passed and, in 2012, became the pretext for Health and Human Service's announcement that the Church was to be forced to violate its principles and support the funding of contraception and abortion. The bishops were outraged:

> We cannot - we will not - comply with this unjust law. People of faith cannot be made second class citizens. We are already joined by our brothers and sisters of all faiths and many others of good will in this important effort to regain our religious freedom. Our parents and grandparents did not come to these shores to help build America's cities and towns, its infrastructure and institutions, its enterprise and culture, only to have their posterity stripped of their God given rights. In generations past, the Church has always been able to count on the faithful to stand up and protect her sacred rights and duties. I hope and trust she can count on this generation of Catholics to do the same. Our children and grandchildren deserve nothing less.[177]

However, this is the logical consequence of a secular, nationalized health care system.

---

[174] Parish bulletin, Church of the Most Holy Trinity," October 18, 2009; the Roman Catholic Church of the Most Holy Trinity is a member of PICO's *San Diego Organizing Project*.
[175] USCCB News Release, "Cardinal Rigali Urges House Committee to Support Pro-Life Amendments to Health Care Reform Bill," July 30, 2009
[176] United States Conference of Catholic Bishops (USCCB) letter, 10-8-09.
[177] Bishop Thomas J. Olmsted, Diocese of Phoenix, Letter read at Sunday Masses, 1-25-12.

The background of Reverend Jim Wallis and his contribution to the founding of *Faith in Public Life* has been described above.[178] Among other things, *Faith in Public Life* created a state-by-state picture of progressivism by means of an interactive map on its website. The nearly 3000 groups identified by *Faith in Public Life* could be contacted by those in the media for a progressive perspective. They had the progressive imprimatur.

Who were these groups? First, there were the faith institutions. Catholics were particularly well represented by diocesan offices around the country and by various chapters of *Catholic Charities, Catholic Relief Services*, and *Catholic Social Services*. Groups that exist to destroy Catholic teaching and Church structure had an impressive presence, too, particularly *Call to Action* and its related *Pax Christi* and *Dignity* chapters. Liberal factions of Jews, Methodists, Evangelicals, Presbyterians, Lutherans, and Muslims were also identified.

Secondly, there were the organizers. Among the *Faith in Public Life* progressives were hundreds of faith-based organizations, all of them related to the organizational theories of Saul Alinsky, and their members.

Lastly, there were the "allies," the secular organizations that have, over the years, contributed to the "vision." Among these were dozens of homosexual activism groups, dozens of abortion "rights" groups, the *Children's Defense Fund, The Interfaith Alliance, People for the American Way*, and the *Center for American Values and Public Life*.

To appreciate how this network works together, take the issue of immigration. Whatever one may think about the United States' immigration situation and the most reasonable way to address it, there's little question that progressive interests have an organized response, which they're calling "comprehensive immigration reform."

Days after Arizona signed a 2010 law giving its police and immigration forces a mandate to enforce current illegal immigration statutes, events around the country were planned in protest. These events weren't the product of the undocumented workers themselves but were, rather, the effort of progressive organizations working among religious institutions.

The Church World Service, the National Council of Churches, Sojourners and the National Hispanic Christian Leadership Conference – two groups whose principal leaders are part of the Council on Faith-Based and Neighborhood Partnerships – the Christian Community Development Association, and the political-media network with which they operated, Faith in Public Life, were principal actors in this national effort.[179]

The major Alinskyian community organizations and their local affiliates were part of the network, too. In Dallas, for instance, Dallas Area Interfaith, an Industrial Areas Foundation affiliate, worked with several other religious institutions to support an immigration march in the

---

[178] See the chapter: "Organizing and Funding in other Religious Institutions"
[179] Bob Allen, "Faith leaders protest Arizona's anti-immigration law," *Associated Baptist Press,* 4-27-10.

city that demanded legalization undocumented workers in the US and protested the Arizona law.[180]

In New York City, Queens Congregations United for Action used an already scheduled vigil to protest the unwelcome direction immigration reform is taking. "What is going on in parts of our country is not good," said the pastor of the event's hosting church. "We must work to change unjust laws." Queens Congregations United for Action is the local affiliate of PICO.[181]

Yet another Alinskyian organizing network, the Gamaliel Foundation, was instrumental in Milwaukee-area immigration protests. At an earlier event that called for an end to deportation and detention, "[s]ome in the crowd chanted 'Si Se Puede,' Spanish for 'Yes, it can be done' – a rallying cry of Cesar Chavez and a slogan of President Barack Obama's campaign…"[182]

In fact, the home page of the Gamaliel Foundation website, as accessed on May 3, 2010, read: "More than 300 Gamaliel Network Clergy and Leaders from across the nation continue Gamaliel's Prayer Vigils for Fair Immigration Reform."

Is this orchestrated?

Of course it is. When, during the 2008 presidential election, the Republican vice-presidential nominee, Sarah Palin, made the remark, "...a small-town mayor is sort of like a community organizer, except that you have actual responsibilities," organizers were furious. Sojourners' Jim Wallis, quoting an outraged organizer who had emailed him in response, blogged, "Community organizers are now most focused in the faith community, working with tens of thousands of pastors and laypeople in thousands of congregations around the country. Faith-based organizing is the critical factor in many low-income communities in the country's poorest urban and rural areas, and church leaders are often the biggest supporters of community organizers."[183]

Let's put the pieces together: Organizers from similar training backgrounds have set up similar sorts of organizational networks around the country, operating

> *Organizers from similar training backgrounds have set up similar sorts of organizational networks around the country, operating within thousands of religious institutions. An organizer, trained by these same folks, becomes the US president. Suddenly, all the Alinskyian organizing networks are working on parallel paths for the same issues, mobilizing their member churches to provide a "moral garment" for each issue (that's an Alinskyian principle for organizing – cloak every issue in a "moral garment") and a turnout of people, chanting the right slogans…. in truth, there's really only one, extremely well-organized response.*

---

[180]   Dianne Solis, "Religious leaders declare support for Dallas immigration march," Dallas News, 4-30-10.
[181]   Nate Schweber, "Queens Vigil Protests Arizona Immigration Law," NY Times, 5-2-10.
[182]   Matthew Olson, "Crowd 'fired up' for change," Kenosha News, 4-29-10.
[183]   Jim Wallis, "Palin Owes Some Good People an Apology," God's Politics Blog, 9-5-08.

within thousands of religious institutions. An organizer, trained by these same folks, becomes the US president. Suddenly, all the Alinskyian organizing networks are working on parallel paths for the same issues, mobilizing their member churches to provide a "moral garment" for each issue (that's an Alinskyian principle for organizing – cloak every issue in a "moral garment") and a turnout of people, chanting the right slogans.

Then the media all around the country picks up the story, usually expressed in local terms that disguise the magnitude of what's happening. Newspaper articles may make it sound as though there's a spontaneous outpouring of grassroots responses to the Arizona immigration law but in truth, there's really only one, extremely well-organized response.

And your congregation may be part of it.

What's it all about? The pertinent aspect of this organizational effort, aside from the spiritual impoverishment it betrays, is its use of the wealth and "moral capital," that is, the respect and influence that religious institutions have in the US, for political purposes – for specifically left-wing politics.

> *The pertinent aspect of this organizational effort, aside from the spiritual impoverishment it betrays, is its use of the wealth and "moral capital," that is, the respect and influence that religious institutions have in the US, for political purposes – for specifically left-wing politics.*

With over 150 homosexual-activist organizations, *Faith In Public Life* has helped shape the message about same-sex "marriage" around the country under a banner of "pro-family values" and "civil rights"…and to leave the impression that this is something "people of faith" can embrace.

With groups like the *Minnesota Religious Coalition for Reproductive Choice* – an organization that "seeks to ensure that every woman is free to make decisions about having children according to her own conscience and religious beliefs" – *Faith In Public Life* will be fighting any opposition to legal abortion from the churches.

With groups like the dozens of *Pax Christi* chapters representing the "moral voice", *Faith In Public Life* will be an advocate for expansion of international governance.

With faith-based community organizations rallying progressive congregations, *Faith In Public Life* will be changing religious institutions into "mediating" institutions between government and its citizens. Every participating congregation will eventually reflect some variant of liberationist theology.

One reviewer for a book on the liberal politics of mainline churches makes two sanguine observations.[184] The first is that all liberally-minded mainline denominations are in decline. The second is that the political threat of conservative Christianity is vastly over-rated as most

---

[184] Review of Diana Butler Bass, *Christianity for the Rest of Us:How the Neighborhood Church Is Transforming the Faith (*Harper San Francisco) by Mark Tooley, *The Weekly Standard*, November 13, 2006.

conservative churches are not focused on politics. He may be right on both counts, and there is no comfort in either observation.

In the preceding pages, we've looked at some of the tactics that Alinskyian organizations use to push the progressive agenda by making it *look* as though there's strong, popular support for what they want. They do that several ways:

One is by **misrepresentation**, by claiming that everyone in their member congregations (or groups) support their work – that they represent ALL the individuals within their member institutions. Is St. James parish a member of Local City Interfaith? If so, then Local City Interfaith will tell the newspaper and the city council that there are 2000 people – the number of congregants in St. James – backing whatever it wants. The truth, however, is that Local City Interfaith will only get 50 of them to its rallies. The other 1950 people who attend St. James have no conscious connection whatsoever to Local City Interfaith.

In *Reveille for Radicals*, Alinsky writes about the effectiveness of what he called "popular participation," the civic actions of ordinary people through a People's Organization.

A critical study of the extent of popular participation in People's Organizations was made, and the findings differed so radically from the prevalent assumptions that the original study was repeatedly checked. Each checkup corroborated the original findings. Conclusions showed that in the most powerful and deeply rooted People's Organizations known in this country the degree of popular participation reached a point of between 5 and 7 per cent! This in spite of the fact that those making the study fully recognized that the organizations being evaluated were so much stronger and included so many more people who actually participate than all the other organizations proclaiming 100 per cent participation...

> *If Alinsky is correct, than 5% involvement of congregations within a denomination can change an entire diocese. A small number of a region's institutions, acting together, can have a tremendous impact on that area. And similarly, a relatively small number of strategically situated, networked affiliates across the country can have a strong influence on federal policy.*

The assumption that Alinsky is debunking in this passage is that an effective organization requires most of its membership to participate. It doesn't. A small, well-organized core of people can accomplish a lot.

Consider what a small percentage Alinsky is describing: 5-7%. 5% of a parish of 5000 is 250 people. Each participating parish requires only a relatively small, committed core of active, involved people to transform that parish. If Alinsky is correct, than 5% involvement of congregations within a denomination can change an entire diocese. A small number of a region's institutions, acting together, can have a tremendous impact on that area. And similarly, a relatively small number of strategically situated, networked affiliates across the country can have a strong influence on federal policy.

Then there is the problem that information is presented in pleasant **sound bytes**. Even among those who attend rallies and actions, one can argue that not many of them understand what they're supporting. DART's Miami-based affiliate had its educational projects – including a program to mentor new teachers – ratified by several thousand participants (allegedly representing about 37 institutions) at its action assembly. Who wouldn't support mentoring new teachers? Who doesn't applaud improving education?

It's unlikely that many of those participants read the program or knew that, among other things, its purpose included helping new "teachers prepare standard-based lesson plans by utilizing student achievement data."[185] It's unlikely that, even among those who *did* read that passage, there was much understanding about what "standard-based lesson plans" signify or what actually is collected in "student achievement data." And yet…that's what all those people were supporting.

Still another Alinskyian tactic is the **accountability meeting** that eschews civic debate in favor of highly orchestrated assemblies that simply allow politicians to publicly ratify or reject the organization's agenda.

Still another tactic is **meeting manipulation**. There was a good example of this in 2002, at a San Antonio National Convocation of Catholic Small Christian Communities (SCCs).

SCCs were the creation of progressives in the United States who hoped to replicate the successes of Latin American base communities. The base communities had been used to pull people away from the Church and teach them Marxist analyses.

In the United States however, a number of Call to Action-associated academics discovered that the SCCs not only tended to retain strong connections to their home parishes but fostered individuals who knew and embraced Church teaching more readily than the general Catholic population.

To correct this "problem," they convened a conference with the stated mission of making the SCCs more socially aware and engaged in activism.

Each of the conference speakers said, in various ways, how important it was for people to link their SCCs to an Alinskyian community organization. There was also guided scripture reflection during which it was explained that a SCC can't be just about fellowship and scripture study. It also has to be about serving the larger community, although "service" didn't mean "feeding the hungry" – it meant joining an Alinskyian organization.

On the last day, participants were divided into five "caucuses" and asked to come up with at three responses for the question: "What do we now see as the major work to foster the

---

[185] Mentoring and Induction for New Teachers (MINT), Miami-Dade County Public Schools Professional Development, undated.

development of SCCs?" In one caucus, participants wanted better Bible studies, more prayer ideas, and offered suggestions for doing works of mercy but, as this wasn't what the conference was intended to promote, the facilitator finally insisted that her caucus include the idea that SCCs join community organizations, too.

She was the only person in the room with that concern and yet it became one of the caucus' three responses and later a "convocation priority" that conference participants were instructed to "ratify."

That's a neat example of Alinskyian manipulation, in which people are used to make it look as though they support something the organizers want. This tactic is the cornerstone of Alinskyian organizing.

Do the radical progressives need a good showing of support for education reform? Alinskyian organizing can produce the *appearance* of that support.

Do they want universal health care? A certain kind of immigration reform? Alinskyian organizing can rally the progressive churches, get out the media, and stage what appears to be a populist uprising.

> *Alinskyian organizing can rally the progressive churches, get out the media, and stage what appears to be a populist uprising.*

Another tactic that seems to confuse people is that the progressives put **layers of organizations between the issues**.

For example: If you were to ask PICO United Florida its position on same-sex marriage, it will insist that it's not concerned about the issue, pro or con. The idea is that, even if someone were to be opposed to redefining marriage, it shouldn't prevent him or her from working with PICO United Florida.

However, PICO United Florida belongs to a coalition called Orange Rising and the Orange Rising Coalition is *very* engaged in creating social change, supporting a local "Tax Equity Ordinance." This ordinance was described by another coalition member as an "aggressive" effort toward moving the state to full "marriage equality."

One problem progressives have faced in the past is that not many people buy into the complete package. Catholics might – as a demographic – approve of properly realized universal healthcare but not recognize abortion "rights." To address this, Alinskyian organizations **scramble the hierarchy of issues**.

To continue with the example of PICO United Florida, the group has worked State Senator Darren Michael Soto with to stop housing foreclosures. While this may be a perfectly unobjectionable local goal, the fact is, Senator Soto is a progressive politician. He's a big supporter of Planned Parenthood. He wants same-sex "marriage" legalized.

PICO's working with Senator Soto gives him political leverage. PICO doesn't have to "endorse" him to *support* him. When he's photographed, flanked at a press conference by PICO United Florida, the message is: "This is our guy. This is a fellow our members can support…even if they disagree with him about other issues. Housing Foreclosure is what's important!"

Pro-life congregations within the Alinskyian organization end up supporting politicians who advance a political agenda that includes the entire spectrum of progressive positions, even if the Alinskyian organization isn't expressing support for abortion.

To take another example, the IAF affiliate *Albuquerque Interfaith* has many religious congregations among its members. However, not all faith-based organizations are equal. There is a tremendous moral rift between those adhering to the truths on which they were founded and those who have abandoned their traditions for more convenient, consensus-driven positions. Among *Albuquerque Interfaith's* members one finds congregations from both camps.

A recent full-page ad in the *Albuquerque Journal* favoring religious recognition of same-sex "marriage" listed over half of Albuquerque Interfaith's congregations as signatories.[186]

Another action in contradiction to traditional moral understanding and common-sense compassion has been the effort to block a local fetal pain ordinance[187] that would have introduced *some* measure of consideration for the sentient child in the womb. This is not a popular position for pro-abortionists. Under the banner of *Respect Albuquerque Women*, the *American Civil Liberties Union, Young Women United, Planned Parenthood of the Rocky Mountains, National Organization for Women* (Santa Fe), *New Mexico Religious Coalition for Reproductive Choice*, the state *League of Women Voters*, and others[188] fought the potential ban.

Respect Albuquerque Women began its campaign with press conference and kickoff event on August 1, 2012.[189] It was held at La Mesa Presbyterian Church whose senior pastor, Trey Hammond, is co-chair of *Albuquerque Interfaith*. Other prominent *Albuquerque Interfaith* supporters, Jerry Ortiz y Pino and Rev. James (Jim) Collie, a representative of the Presbytery of Santa Fe (PSUSA), were signatories of a MoveOn.org "We stand with Albuquerque women" petition against the ban.

The point is not that *Albuquerque Interfaith* or any of the hundreds of other Alinskyian faith-based organizations around the United States are *directly* promoting same-sex "marriage" or abortion "rights" but that these are political organizations[190] in which morally-respectful religious institutions are politically yoked to morally-unhinged religious institutions. The irony of this arrangement, sadly, is that instead of the *moral* factor acting as a yeast for the betterment of society, which it would do if it held firm to its values – *immoral* factors gain leverage,

---

[186] Ad: "We Are Faith Leaders and We Support the **freedom to marry** in New Mexico," (emphasis in the original), *Albuquerque Journal,* October 9, 2013.

[187] The Pain Capable Unborn Child Protection Ordinance which is slated for a citywide run-off election on November 19, to be voted on by Albuquerque residents.

[188] The group hosting an October 9, 2013 *Respect Albuquerque Women* meeting is *Self Serve*, an adult "toy store." Need one say more? www.dukecityfix.com/events/respect-albuquerque-women-conversation?xg_source=activity

[189] *Albuquerque Center for Peace and Justice* calendar: http://ww.abqpeaceandjustice.org/index.php/calendar/event/3/jao1m398shls40qkl8uel8s2og

[190] As an example of its partisan nature, *Albuquerque Interfaith* gave money to the *Obama for America* campaign. Federal Election Commission, Report of Contribution by Employer to the *Obama for America*, primary election, filed 11/21/2011: query.nictusa.com/pres/2008/M5/C00431445/A_EMPLOYER_C00431445.html

neutralizing that "yeast." Why? Because the moral factor has said, in effect, that its *moral* position is less important than its *corporate* position.

So, although the Archbishop of Santa Fe has issued a press release in favor of the *Pain Capable Unborn Child Protection Ordinance* (later-term abortion ban),[191] it has gone little further than the Archdiocese's website. Its position on same-sex "marriage" has been better publicized but is diluted in the face its allies' far grander public campaigns.

The moral position in such circumstances becomes a little…awkward. The prudential issues, by contrast, take on a disproportionate importance. Shorn of their moral strength, the more "traditional" members of the Alinskyian organizations are shocked that the healthcare legislation they supported in "a relationship of trust" with their fellow Alinskyians suddenly is discovered to include abortion funding and mandates for contraceptive provision, or that compulsory government-controlled education requires even parochial schools to include "sex education" or "tolerance" training. But it's a predictable and logical consequence of an unequal yoking of institutions.

Alinskyian organizations have only one goal: the furthering of progressive political and social ends. Any institution within its alliance – regardless of its individual positions – serves the ends of the alliance, not the individual.

> *Alinskyian organizations have only one goal: the furthering of progressive political and social ends. Any institution within its alliance – regardless of its individual positions – serves the ends of the alliance, not the individual.*

---

[191] Archbishop Michael J. Sheehan, Press Release: "Later Term Abortion Ban," 9-27-13.

Charitable "practice" has been honed by people of faith for 2000 years. In the western world, congregations of believers, Christian and Jewish, reached out to their neediest members as well as to other needy congregations.

The early Church understood that Christ intended Christian charity to include people outside the Christian family. The *Didache,* written around100 AD, is a brief text of instructions for Christians that contains the exhortation to "give to everyone who asks thee, and do not refuse." The Roman Emperor Julian (361 to 363 AD) wrote: "The impious Galileans relieve both their own poor and ours . . . . It is shameful that ours should be so destitute of our assistance."[192]

> *The 20th century saw a perversion of Christian charity that sought to create a utopian "system" rather than provide a personal work of love. One sees this in the writing of Jack Jezreel, the founder of JustFaith, a program to evangelize within Christian communities for exactly this utopian "system."*

Not only did congregations and wealthy individuals make generous provision for all manner of need but religious congregations were established to perform particular charitable acts in an organized way. The Alexian Brothers were formed, in part, as a response to the devastation of the Black Death, nursing the sick and burying the dead despite personal risk.

Convent (monastic) schools trained young boys in reading and writing from all economic backgrounds. The Order of the Blessed Virgin Mary of Mercy was founded to ransom slaves. St. John Bosco organized the Salesians to educate and train poor children for future employment.

These are some of the finest examples – the "best practices," if you will – of Christian charity. They demonstrate practical, self-sacrificing, and generous concern for other people that was personal and effective, on spiritual as well as material levels.

The 20th century saw a perversion of Christian charity that sought to create a utopian "system" rather than provide a personal work of love. One sees this in the writing of Jack Jezreel, the founder of JustFaith, a program to evangelize within Christian communities for exactly this utopian "system."

In a recent article, Jezreel articulates the subtle twist he has given to Christian charity. For one thing, he wants the congregation to put all its resources - its "preaching, teaching, adult education, youth ministry, children's catechesis, everything" – into pushing Christians to engage in "direct service, advocacy, community organizing, and sacrificial giving."[193]

---

[192] *Epistles of Julian*, 49
[193] Jack Jezreel, "Best Practices for Charity and Justice," *U.S. Catholic*, 3-14.

This is an interesting comment. In the first place, for two millennia, Christendom has accomplished heroic acts of charity that fundamentally changed human society without creating a propaganda machine. People acted out of love.

Charity, as a free act of love, is an ancient concept. Tertullian, writing his *Apology* in the early 200s, speaks of a "treasure-chest" of money for the poor kept in the Christian community. "On the monthly day, if he likes, each puts in a small donation; but only if it be his pleasure, and only if he be able: for there is no compulsion; all is voluntary."

In the second place, Jezreel's list of "charitable acts" contains two novel elements bookended by traditional works. Christians have always recognized the importance of "direct service" – what we used to call "works of mercy" – and "sacrificial giving" (alms). "Community organizing" and "advocacy," however, are new additions that serve the utopian gods but have scant usefulness otherwise.

There doesn't need to be a restructuring of the parish to persuade Christians that the soup kitchen needs to be staffed; however, a great deal of reeducation is essential to persuade them to join the local Alinskyian Interfaith and the abortion-dealing healthcare legislation it promotes.

Jezreel goes on to say that "there's a large body of work to be done" and those working to help the homeless aren't in competition with those working to provide communities with clean drinking water. That's quite true.

> *Charity, as a free act of love, is an ancient concept. Tertullian, writing his Apology in the early 200s, speaks of a "treasure-chest" of money for the poor kept in the Christian community. "On the monthly day, if he likes, each puts in a small donation; but only if it be his pleasure, and only if he be able: for there is no compulsion; all is voluntary."*

But political advocacy and Alinskyian community organizing aren't ministries. Sometimes, they aren't even ethical. So, when Jezreel writes that without "enough social ministry opportunities, the great potential in many parishes goes untapped" we see a secular vision. The parish is a resource to be "tapped" by an idealistic social engineer with big plans.

"Advocacy" and "community organizing" don't address "structural causes of problems" from a *Christian* perspective. They approach "structural causes of problems" from a *secular* perspective, seeking to change "bad" economic systems and "bad" governance according the latest intellectual fashions. In classic utopian style, the cart is before the horse and, ironically, the actual "structural causes of problems" can never be addressed because one is

> *So, when Jezreel writes that without "enough social ministry opportunities, the great potential in many parishes goes untapped" we see a secular vision. The parish is a resource to be "tapped" by an idealistic social engineer with big plans.*

trying to "fix" the wrong "structure."

The "best practice" of charity is a life freely laid down for another; the worst is "breaking a few eggs to make an omelet." In the former, one *imitates* God; in the latter, one *plays* God.

There's an abyss between the two.

About the Author

Stephanie Block is the author of *Change Agents: Alinskyian Organizing among Religious Bodies*, a four-volume series that details many of the points made in *Organizing the Culture of Death*. Volume I concerns the history of Alinskyian organizing, volume II the primary issues such organizing addresses, volume III the ideology behind Alinskyian organizing, and volume IV looks at politics and objections.

She is also a contributor at Spero News (www.speroforum.com), covering topics related to social justice and contemporary assaults against human life.

Made in the USA
Coppell, TX
06 November 2020